MARIA CLARA LUCCHETTI BINGEMER

A Face for God

Translated by Jovelino Ramos
and Joan Ramos

CONVIVIUMPRESS

SERIES TRADITIO

2014

A Face for God

http://www.conviviumpress.com
sales@conviviumpress.com
ventas@conviviumpress.com
convivium@conviviumpress.com

7661 NW 68th St, Suite 108
Miami, Florida 33166. USA
Phone: +1 (305) 8890489
Fax: +1 (305) 8875463

Edited by Rafael Luciani
Translated by Jovelino Ramos and Joan Ramos
Revised by Doris and Tom Strieter
Designed by Eduardo Chumaceiro d'E
Series: *Traditio*

ISBN: 978-1-934996-54-6

Printed in Colombia
Impreso en Colombia
Panamericana Formas e Impresos S.A.

Convivium Press
Miami, 2014

A Face for God

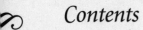 *Contents*

Introduction

Nothing to Ask You

Today I have
nothing to ask you
Neither do I bring you
any complaint.
I only look for
an encounter
from the infinite
that pulsates in me.
Poor me
if I tied
your answer
to my measured
question
or to my hurt
lament!
Poor me
if I already knew
the answer!
Perhaps
I might find
for my thirst
only my own
recycled water,
the echo
of my monotonous
self talk,
my past
moistened
by sweat
or by weeping.
I need you
well beyond

what I know
what I say
about myself.
Today I discover,
already present,
in the love
with which you attract me,
the passion
with which you search for me! 🐦

Benjamín González Buelta, SJ

Since the world has been the world, and since humankind tried its first steps on earth, the human being has been searching for the face of God. Men and women of all times and places —the only living beings for whom reality neither begins nor ends in their own senses and instincts, and the only ones who believe that the horizon goes well beyond the reach of their gaze— desire and ardently yearn for a glimpse of the face of the mystery that they feel and assume as a presence in their lives.

Our age is not very different from the preceding ones. Yet it has some particularities regarding the way or direction by which, and for what purpose, it performs this search for vision and understanding of the face and mystery of God in human history.

The world we live in is not like the world of our ancestors. We are not surrounded by symbols, signs and affirmations of the Christian —and especially the Catholic— faith. Today religion more often plays the role of a culture and civilizing force than that of a creed of adherence that configures life. Furthermore, we live in a world which is plural in all its aspects and fashions. Such pluralism, enhanced by globalization, affects not only economic and social, but equally political, cultural and religious contexts. Today people are born and grow up in a world where on the one hand they intersect, interact and dialogue with atheism, unbelief and/or religious indifference, and on the other, with new and ancient religions that cross-fertilize each other. Historical Christianity finds itself in the middle of this plurality and cross-fertilization.

Such religious pluralism, for its part, implies the existence of discourse and attempts at discourse about the sacred, the Divine or God, reflecting the characteristic contexts they come from. Such discourse will be pervaded and even configured, to a greater or lesser extent, by the phenomenon of secularization that drives and transforms the vision of the religious and cultural contexts, as well as by the emergence of somewhat conflicted relationships among different religions —not only those with the most ancient and institutionalized traditions, but also the new religious movements that every day invent new syntheses to express today's search for God and the naming of God.

The reflections presented in this book are an attempt to identify, from the standpoint of Christian theology, some of the traits that compose the face —the identifiable profile— of the God of the Christian faith. In line with that we shall try to envisage how the Christian concept of God approaches and comprehends this mystery, without ignoring the questions that arise today in thinking and talking about this God. Among other things we shall try to perceive how these traits that, in our view, identify the face of the Christian God, «interface» with other traits, overlapping at the level of dialogue and communication and proposing new and unsuspected syntheses to the generations of the Twenty-First Century. Finally we shall try to identify some of the consequences and challenges for theology brought and planted by these faces and interfaces in the soil of the theological scene.

The chapters here presented are in part original and in part previously published work. That being the case, in the concluding bibliography we will list the publications from which the material was taken and offered here as a new synthesis. Moreover we would like to mention two recent works written in partnership with Professor, Doctor and Father Vitor Feller that to a great extent inspired the writing of some chapters, especially chapter 9. They are *Deus Trindade: a vida no coração do mundo,* SP, Paulinas, 2000, and *Deus Amor: graça que habita em nós,* SP, Paulinas, 2002. Here, then, our expression of gratitude to this companion and co-author, hoping that the reader will be aware of his considerable role in the construction of these reflections.

We introduce this book with the joy of a somewhat unusual partner: poetry. As someone who for quite a while has been engaged in an interdisciplinary effort with theology and literature, we surely understand with growing vigor that theology as much as poetry owes its origin and existence to the winds of inspiration, of which we don't know where it comes from or where it goes. That's why we decided to place at the introduction of each chapter a psalm-poem by my spiritual master and friend Father Benjamin González Buelta, SJ, spanish jesuit that lives in Cuba and an «untiring singer» of God's mystery[1]. We hope that the beauty of his verses will introduce the reader with enhanced enthusiasm and openness to our reflections. They are expected to be respectful and serious reflections. But we are also fully and humbly aware of their limits and insufficiency before the Sanctity of this God who showed his face and said his name in the midst of history and who didn't wish to be identified by any other name but Love.

If the reading of this book turns out to be a small exercise of introduction to the dynamics of this love, I believe its main objective will have been fulfilled.

Rio de Janeiro, April 20th, 2014
Easter Sunday

---

1   The psalms by Father González Buelta quoted here can be found with many others in «Salmos para sentir e saborear as coisas internamente. Uma ajuda para a experiência dos Exercícios Espirituais», Juiz de Fora, Publicações Monásticas, 2004. *English edition:* GONZÁLEZ BUELTA S.J., Benjamín, *Psalms to accompany the Spiritual Exercises of St Ignatius of Loyola*, (translated by Damian Howard S.J.), The Way, Oxford 2012.

A Profile for God?

1

Mystery Every Where

The enquiry of the atheist,
the believer's prayer,
a growing love,
a tale grown weary,
one day come up
against silence,
as the only answer
to the mystery.

When we, the impatient ones,
cannot bear
the silence of the mystery,
we turn the cross into a sword,
the crescent moon into a cutlass;
we compare the waters of the Jordan
and the Ganges,
as ritual ablutions,
and we cling to the catechism
like a pass to an exclusive club.
When we cannot bear
the silence of mystery,
we deny ourselves birthings
in night-time,
or in difference,
aborting
questions and prayers,
fondness and fables.

Still, all human enquiry,
every true unease,
of whatever hue,

is a scattering of seed
in the silence
like the sowing of rice
between earth and water.
From out of the mystery,
at the ordained moment, will sprout
nourishment for all,
and it will not trouble to ask
which creed sowed it
or who its owner really is.

It has so many defenders,
and so many credit cards,
this knowledge of the mystery,
that all we have left
is the «not knowing» of silence
before God and between ourselves:
the best soil there is
for sowing together
the seeds of a more humane future.

If we cannot
affirm the mystery together,
then together we can implore it,
and, together, await
its reply.

BENJAMÍN GONZÁLEZ BUELTA, SJ *(p. 12)*

Perhaps it might be simple to enumerate in a few pages the attributes and characteristics of the God worshiped by the Christian faith, naming or invoking this God as Father, Son and Holy Spirit. More than twenty centuries of church history and theology certainly provide an abundance of uncontested material on orthodoxy, allowing us to accomplish this task at possible and sufficient levels of adequacy. Yet the ineffability of God's mystery would lead us to an unsurmountable point where our poor human language would confess itself incapable of describing that which happens only at the profoundest depths of the human being: the experience of this God.

Yet this experience is the unavoidable pathway to the knowledge of this same God, a pathway that is not purely theoretical. This knowledge wouldn't risk even touching the true nucleus of God's being, existence and moves. In this book, therefore, we shall try to identify the question of God —and very concretely the God of Christianity— in this moment of crisis of paradigms and civilizing models. We shall also try to perceive the challenge posed to modern society —both agnostic and pluri-religious— in its interaction with this question, which continues to be the greatest of all questions.

We shall try to follow the ways through which the people of Israel and the early church were continually finding the profile, the contours and the naming of their God, and then proceed with the search and final pursuit of whatever clues arise, whether from the experience, from the practice which results from the clues and is enriched by them, or from theological reflection.

2

God: A Primordial Question

The current situation of Christianity, and therefore the theme of God, could in part be summarized as follows: after the prevailing conviction that other religions or religious traditions gravitated around Christianity, which for centuries was seen as the center of world religious phenomena, it is well past the time for us to acknowledge that the center of gravity for all religious traditions, including Christianity, is God.

The concept of GOD, or the Transcendent, or the Ultimate Reality, is considered fundamental by all religious systems, since it gives meaning to the world in general and to human life in particular. The authentic religious question then, in spite of the process of modernity, the crisis of secularization and other phenomena more or less analyzed by the great commentators, continues to be that which asks precisely what is it to which human beings can authentically give the name of GOD.

One of the pretensions of modernity has been to push away the question of God from the horizons of humankind. To that effect it has been said that secularization is just the active or passive process of returning to the *saecumlum*, that is, the profane world, away from a reality strictly linked to God and religion. Modernity and secularization would then be deeply synchronized, leading to a positive value judgement if a secularized civilization were considered superior to those that are not secularized. The former would be the civilization of rationality, of emancipation at all levels, where a mature humankind wouldn't need any longer a Supreme Being, an Absolute, to dictate the norms of conduct and organization.

The crisis of modernity, rather than bringing this process to an end, assumes its main characteristics and aims at radicalizing the cultural and conceptual «death» of God. Along with the reappearance of the religious, atheism did not disappear from the western horizon. This is no longer just any atheism, nor is it a pure and simple lack of religion. It is a religious indifference that doesn't care at all for any reasoning about the existence or non-existence of God.

Basically, the modern era professes the disappearance of God and of all traits of God's existence. Even more: while modern atheism denied God and affirmed a human project —God's death would be the price to be paid so that human autonomy and freedom could emerge and develop fully— contemporary postmodern atheism and religious indifference threaten to debunk humanism once and for all by questioning the existence and coherence of the foundations of society and the globality of the real.

Not wishing to inherit anything from the death of God, contemporary atheism is not the atheism of expropriation and re-appropriation from believer to non-believer, from the religious to the secular, from faith in God to faith in man. It remains tied to a nostalgia and to other «truer» values as well as to other «more authentic» cultures.

Postmodern thinking, characterized by the «deconstruction» and relativization of the apparently solid conceptual edifice of modernity, also questions all attempts to approach the ineffable Absolute that Christians and other religious traditions call God. It considers any discourse aiming at universalization and totalization as reductionist, inadequate, and leading to indifference and disenchantment. That being the case, it opens an apparently new, but actually very old, avenue to Christian discourse and thinking, which leads to the mystery and to pluralism as a confession of the impossibility of our complete comprehension and expression of any aspect of the Being.

It follows that not only reason and reflection, but also the desire and thirst for the infinite and for transcendence, find themselves cornered in a perplexity which could have the opposite effect of trust and of amazement before the Mystery. And the result, although inverted and paradoxical, could be that the experience and discourse regarding God might find, in the course of these apparently hostile times, a surprising possibility of fertility.

If the objectivity of the world —the fruit of modernity— is the extreme result of the separation from God, a separation that liberates human beings and makes them subjects of their knowledge, and thus autonomous before the divine intelligence and norms, then the problem can be considered from another angle. This would be the supreme foundation of things as God delivered and —to use the language of faith— revealed them to the human intellect, even if in a barely perceptible and intimately accessible way, and even if only partially. And now God, or Transcendence —according to the modern conception— withdraws, leaving human beings prey to their work and contentions. Religion and the experience of God would, therefore, be conceived as a discourse of human beings about God with the objective of defining the relationship between them and God, and also as a sequence of world views.

Today, at the moment when we are living and dealing with the painful crisis of modernity or the advent of the postmodernity, it is possible for us to understand a little better this conception. All the ways of talking about God have unraveled and their radical unsuitability is constantly highlighted. The radical experience of the mystery questions a modern discourse aimed at throwing light on everything, including the «withdrawal» or the «death» of God. The relativization of all cultural premises and the critique of the modern project alert us to rushed and badly handled approaches that could include a discourse about God with intent to legitimize all institutionalizations and systems.

The demise of anthropocentric humanism (with its perverse androcentric and ethnocentric connotations) makes possible a new vision and a new perception —which consequently becomes a new experience— of a deity, still not clearly detectable or namable, which allows its seductive and attractive power to be understood, even if only in a discretely veiled way, and provokes a desire to have this experience.

It would not be fitting to accept the premise that we live in a time of weakening for both faith in God and reflection about God. Even if we take into account that the modern era has proclaimed the inevitable decline of religion —and the thesis of the death of Go— the identification of modernity with atheistic humanism carries with it an unsustainable reductionism. Indeed, the project of modernity engendered religious indifference before the negation of God. At the same time, the crisis of such a project demonstrated that, unless it finds its foundation in God, a society will inexorably unravel itself. Correctly or not, no matter how well grounded, the proclamation of the advent of so-called postmodernity and of the supposed «return» of the religious allows us to see how inadequate it is to decree the banishment of God from the human horizon. On the contrary, the search for God continues to agitate the heart of humankind, notwithstanding the risk run by all «official» or officious discourses about God (in a number of institutions), of discovering themselves —as was the case with some of them— to be hopelessly out of date.

To summarize, if atheism, as understood in modern terms, continues to be a question that arises with the mention of the problem of God, one has to acknowledge that such a question is no longer unique, and probably recognizes atheism, if not as a contribution, at least as a presence in modern culture. Indeed this culture is fully immersed in pluralism and facing the new challenge of understanding its own identity and the identity of the God that one proposes to announce and to serve.

3
The Question of God in Contemporary Brazil

In Brazil, it is as easy to find many reflections of the world situation as just described, as it is to perceive new and original elements appropriate to the local situation. Recent research and published material show that in spite of the arrival of modernity with its baggage of atheism and secularization, we continue to be a fundamentally religious country, where the pursuit of the encounter with God is part of daily life.

Given the current situation of economic crisis and the extreme poverty of the Brazilian people, divine power —that is, God— emerges as the only source of salvation and liberation from all evils. This is especially true for the fundamentalist denominations of pronounced biblicism, such as the pentecostals, whose accelerated growth is quite a concern for the historical churches.

It is, therefore, easy to see that the issue of modernity and its crisis, no matter how great its space in the Brazilian religious field, do not manage to eclipse the problem of God or to diminish the strength of its questioning, which is still very much alive and vibrant. Similarly, socioeconomic and political factors would no longer be, as in the past, the major —or the watershed— point of the question. In other words, one cannot affirm that the thirst and search for God in Brazilian society is a privilege of the poor and the popular classes, while leaving atheism, agnosticism or advanced secularism as an option for the dominant or educated classes.

It is no longer acceptable to affirm, in view of the currently accelerating changes in the Brazilian religious field, that the popular or poor classes are uniformly and deeply religious while the other classes are irremediably affected and disturbed by modernity and its fruits.

It is important to acknowledge not only that modernity has managed to penetrate Brazil. It brought to Brazil a new synthesis, different from that of the Old World, especially to the new generations. Yet one can still find religious search as well as religious indifference, not only among the poor but also in the affluent classes. If it is true that the most deprived groups of the Brazilian population, especially those in rural areas, to a great extent still live out the purity of Catholicism, it is also true that many of them migrated to, and crowded into, the periphery of the great cities. There they are exposed to the proliferation of new religious propositions that often stifle or cloud the Christian proposition. For their part, many middle class people and groups, as well as many members of the intellectual and academic sectors —coming from a recent past of political militancy and agnosticism— are now engaged in authentic religious search. For them Christianity has a place, but not a primordial, hegemonic or unique one.

All analyses attempting to obtain a clear profile of the Brazilian religious field would then necessarily be simplistic. For this reason we will limit ourselves to enumerating these points without attempting to go further into an area already much scrutinized by social science experts. As we consider Brazilian society and the current situation of religion on the world scene, we do not want to risk digging deeper into a ground which is not ours.

Our discourse proposes to be completely different. We don't want to get away from our area, which is theology. If we have ventured to do some analysis, it was with the intention of establishing our objective from the beginning: to talk about God from a theological perspective. We will try to consider from the theological point of view the questions arising at this time in relation to our concern, namely, the specifics of God in Christianity. With the instrument of theology we will search for answers to these questions, whether in the fields of experience or praxis, or in theological reflection itself, as specific areas of knowledge and thought.

From Seduction to Experience

Karl Rahner, who is considered —and justly so— one of the greatest theologians of the Twentieth Century, said that the Christian of the future (and we should add, of the present as well) would be a mystic, that is, someone who experienced something. Otherwise he or she would be nothing, and certainly not a Christian. As always —and today more than ever— to talk about God from the perspective of the Christian faith means to talk about an experience. Or better yet, it means to talk from the perspective of an experience. Because this experience is deeply divine it is also human, and has been profoundly so since that moment when, in the fullness of time, the Christian faith proclaimed that God became flesh, God became humankind, God became incarnate Word, in Jesus Christ.

Incarnate, human, and therefore particular, this experience is nonetheless universal and total. It is so due to the fact that there is necessarily a relationship that is always particular between the Christian option and its otherness —that which is not part of it, due not to opposition but to excess. This experience can recognize God as the object of its desire and the reason for its existence. To recognize itself as particular and historical is to recognize not only its own existence and its limitations, but also that of the other, the sign of that Other whom none can fully embrace, the always greater God. While there is nothing in the experience of God to be seen or perceived as particular (although there is a participation in a universal visibility and experientiality), this experience is nothing less than seeing, hearing, listening, touching —in a word, experiencing— God. This God is self-revealed and self-manifested through a most limited concreteness —the face, the flesh of the other— and through the historical and social context in which this other lives out his or her incarnate condition and real existence.

If it could be proved, fairly or not, that Christianity had in some way lost the possibility of expressing itself to today's world through the word and proclamation, in a loud and clear voice, regarding the God who is present in the heart of its experience, that would be due on the one hand to the divorce that has slowly developed between the experience and practice of faith, and on the other, to important and meaningful human feelings which can unsettle even what is most noble in human beings. Whenever these structuring and highly meaningful experiences lose their resemblance to Christian experience at personal, community and ecclesial levels, they cease to be productive and salvific. They would no longer deserve to be properly called experiences of God.

At the current moment, religious pluralism and the consequent search for religious dialogue among the religious traditions that are part of it and concerned about it —the traditional Christian churches— find in the experience of God a fertile soil for possible productive work. Regarding experiences at the heart of several religions, we cannot simply reduce one to another or identify one with another, yet it is evident that mystical and religious experience can be a prime ground for a religious and theological dialogue —a dialogue that we hope can lead human beings to face fundamental questions such as: Where did we come from and where are we going? What is the meaning of human existence in view of its burden of suffering and death? What is the source of this movement we share, which places us in relationships, lifts us outside ourselves into solidarity and fellowship with the other, and is itself the answer to the question of an Absolute that we are aware of and believe in? The response to these questions —even if mysterious and veiled— and the simple fact that they disquiet us, highlight the experience of God as Christianity's indispensable criterion not only for enhancing the understanding of its own identity, but also for moving toward the difference that questions us and paradoxically makes us more and more faithful at the center of its fundamental truth.

As a starting point for dialogue in a pluri-religious world, the experience of God represents the possibility for the human being to live out the fundamental anthropological dimension of gratitude. By walking the road of the experience of God, a Christian realizes that the One desired by his or her heart is never found in the immediateness of ones needs, and much less in the frenetic consumerism of some psychological attitudes or in affective conquests. At the level of desire, the experience of God happens only in a spontaneous way, leaving whoever has tried it always unsatisfied and thus always capable of desiring more and, therefore, of trying again and again.

The Judeo-Christian tradition recognizes and assumes the natural presence of desire in the human being. The Scriptures ceaselessly take into account this human desire as grounded in the vehement aspiration for life fulfillment, whose fundamental element lies in the building of a personal relationship with God. Yet this experience does not consist —for Judaism and still less for Christianity— in a permanent satisfaction or free enjoyment of all desires.

If on the one hand «only desire can qualify God's relationship with the human being», on the other the relationship established by this desire places a man or woman before God's «difference»: the difference in desiring the Other when the encounter can take place only through self-renunciation, through conversion and through divestiture of their own desires. In the Christian experience this is the only way to make space for whatever God may desire in the human being, and then to allow the human being to desire nothing except God and to identify that desire more and more with the divine desire. In this experience the human being is taken by God, and not the other way around. And the experience, if real, remains completely out of human control.

If, therefore, the experience of God happens at the level of desire and cannot happen in any other way, it must also be understood that it happens as mystery. It is surely revealed mystery, a mystery of love which comes close to salvific proximity, while remaining always mystery. There is no logical and natural transition between the experience of God and the experience of everyday life, even if this is where it happens. We can talk about an analogical knowledge, based on the fundamental perception that no reality is capable of expressing transcendence. Also, regarding the totality of the human experience of transcendence, the word mystery best defines the discovery of God as the Absolute who attracts and invites us to the experience.

At the level of communication, therefore, silence is more suitable than a word for the experience of God. Silence is the companion of this experience, of the intimate understanding of it, of its enjoyment, and ultimately of the perception that concepts are insufficient to express it. One must become silent to really possess it. There is a mystery of death immanent in human language and consciousness regarding the expression of God, or better, regarding the description of the experience of God as the possibility of knowing the Absolute. This is to acknowledge that all began before the humankind, which arrived, in one way or another, only «posteriorly» and too late to be fully part of the Mystery or in full relationship with it.

Yet, the incarnation of the Word in Jesus of Nazareth says to the Christian that, by the sheer grace and mercy of God, time was granted a new meaning and this «posteriorness» was redeemed. Hence the Christian religious experience consists in the indissoluble union of two apparently (humanly) irreconcilable poles: the theological fact that God consented to be experienced both as Absolute and as father/mother. Defined as love since the first hour of Christianity, this God is revealed as father/mother in the intimate personal relationship with humans. The primordial characterization of this relationship is that of a «loving union established with Jesus of Nazareth, in whom the Christian faith recognized the beloved Son of this always unseen God».

The mystery of God's Incarnation in Jesus Christ reveals not only that the Absolute is experienced by the human being as parenthood, but also that this experience allows a glimpse into a distinctiveness and plurality in the interior of the Being of God, experienced as Father, as Son and as Holy Spirit.

Nowadays the great difficulty in speaking intelligently about the God of Christian revelation to modern, postmodern and/or post-Christian listeners is sometimes due to the fact that for some time historical Christianity paid little attention either to the question of the experience of God or to a pedagogy of such experience. Fearing the intimism and subjectivism generated by modern individualism that could result in alienation as well as historical and communal disengagement —which by and large had already happened, and continues to happen— Christians became impiously suspicious of anything coming from religious experience that had the appearance, no matter how remote, of proximity to the so-called mystical experience. Apparently that should be appropriate only for a half dozen privileged persons, usually headed for a cloistered life of contemplation and having to cope with all kinds of suspicions about their «normality» and «mental health».

It appears that this kind of suspicion has finally begun to wane, and the time has come for Christian churches to seriously deal with the question of the experience of God or see the failure of their mission at this delicate moment in history. Even thinkers more in tune with the nihilism undergirding the modern project are coming, although reluctantly, to the conclusion that an atheistic or nonreligious society cannot provide humankind with answers, or raise other questions without enhancing psychological hopelessness and stress. Which leaves us with the question: Since alienation and illusion are neither the way forward nor desirable objectives for humans —would the alternative be despair, depression or insanity?

5

Divine Action and/or Human Action?

On the other hand, to desire is always to want something, and the highest thing to be desired is happiness. Ethics and moral action express a belief in the possibility of a happy time and space where human beings can reach their full maturity and fully enjoy their potentialities. All in this world that denies this and signals its absence is tantamount to a questioning of both human ethics and human action.

The ethical attitude that the Church calls love (agape) is not contradicted by the experience of God, nor does it negate the affirmation that this God, revealed by grace, is an object of desire but not of need. If human beings, in the givenness of contemplation and in the depth of the experience of God, can feel the proximity of the Absolute Ineffable never seen by anyone, they can also perceive a profundity —related to this One who questions them from the heart of reality— as an authentic manifestation of the divine.

Moreover, it is this dialectical movement of the experience of the infinite in the finite —of the questioning from the heart of the infinite which emerges in ethical behavior— that intervenes in the finite and, transforming it, touches at the same time the fringes of the infinite. It allows humans to assume consciousness of this Absolute who rules their lives with love —the same God who in Jesus Christ reveals God's name as Father. In going to the depths of their poor and limited existence, marked by all kinds of conflicts, injustices and restrictions, human beings assume consciousness of a divine origin, a consciousness which is not part of their common experience or, better said, not part of the knowledge that they would otherwise obtain from such experience.

Today, more than ever, the crisis of modernity makes it imperative for Christians to give God an adoration that must include not only a commitment to serve the neighbor but also an ethical presence and action in the heart of society. This practice could be for Christians a sign from the God of their faith, and much more a sign of what they lack than of what they have in plenty. The insufficiency of favorable means and conditions for the working of this praxis is a testimony to the immensity of its concern and of what gives it structure and meaning. In a world in which fundamental questions are more openly formulated than before; in a world in which the thirst for meaning and for fundamental ethical imperatives is, more than ever, dramatically felt, Christianity is called to reflect in its human action nothing less than divine action.

The guarantee of universality and globalism that makes possible the identification of the divine seal in human praxis paradoxically demands the most insignificant and limited manifestation of its action, that is, serving the poor. Universality without the inclusion of the lowest, the most despised, and the neediest of the world, would be simply another ideology. The guarantee of the authenticity of revelation is not discriminatory, but reflects a preference for the poorest, the most abandoned and the most exploited.

As with all areas of human action, praxis on behalf of the poor —the fundamental requirement of the knowledge and proclamation of the God of Christianity— is free of neither ambiguity nor risk. Specifically, in Latin America, and certainly in Brazil, where this praxis has been an obligatory pursuit by significant sectors of the Church —from clergy to laity— such risks have been more and more felt in the ecclesial experience of recent decades.

This praxis has often been accused —and not always unfairly— of complicity with the most negative contributions of modernity, such as hegemony of power, pride in the presumption of knowledge of history's secret moves and the ability to influence its direction, exacerbation of militancy, as well as feverish activism at the expense of other aspects of the ecclesial life. But the option for the poor nevertheless continues to be an invaluable corrective regarding the risks inherent in a postmodern «evasiveness» that emphasizes original and jubilant thought while giving primacy to sensations —or spontaneous and immediate pleasure— over sentiment.

The ecological, feminist and other movements are not immune to these risks. These movements bring new subjects and questions to a field until recently dominated by the theology of liberation, with its praxis focused on socio-economic and political concerns. In spite of its positive contributions to the Church in Latin America and in the world, this theology is not free from the inherent risks of modernity —of which it is, in a way, a product. Likewise, it appears that it is not exempt from the failure of not having found yet a perfectly adequate theoretical (that is, theological) expression as a basis for its praxis.

This could be due, in part, to the fact that such theoretical —or theological— adequacy can be found only in God, or, better said, in the experience of God —which gives substance and legitimacy to such praxis, while disposing of its ideological temptations and questioning the authenticity of its existence as well as its evangelical radicalism. This is the way to limit the tempting claims which could make praxis acquiescent to the vices of modernity. We believe that a praxis with a firm orientation, responsive to an ethical exigency that emerges from the heart of a disfigured reality, proceeds from the experience of God, as its primal source. This experience will, in addition, be constantly nourished and questioned by the implications of this praxis. If such experience is truly authentic —truly from God— human action will be free from the temptations of pride and power, because it will always reflect the sovereignty of God as guiding the paths of history.

Acting with spontaneity, pursuing proposed objectives, while acknowledging that the greatest objective has already been reached by the incarnation, death and resurrection of Jesus Christ, the Christian will be able to experience and taste the presence of this God —a God of disconcerting and always surprising ways. God's revelation makes evident its own structural inadequacy for each and every political, socioeconomic, cultural (and even religious) model that may have the pretension of expressing it.

Inspiring and interpreting itself in such a way, human action will be in reality the image of divine action, which is indeed its primal source. As a non-logical mystery, and a mystery of salvation (always in the act of liberation, intervening in our reality in a salvific manner) the God of the Christian faith continues self-revealing, now more than ever, as a mystery of love and compassion. God's action, contrary to modern standards of efficacy, does not favor areas of creation whose fruits, at the level of progress, transformation and development, are perceived in more concrete and visible forms. Yet it happens precisely when oppression does its most powerful predatory work, without revealing its creative and divine source. For a dwelling place, it favors spaces and situations in which it can be perceived only indistinctly and *sub specie contraria*. Thus, above and beyond a mystery of compassion, God's action is inspiration for the human praxis that desires to experience and witness God's truth and love.

A God who Listens and Speaks

What Matters Most

What matters most is
not that I seek you
but that you pursue me in all my journeying (Genesis 3: 9)

not that I call you by your name,
but that you have mine tattooed
in the palm of your hand (Isaiah 49: 16)

not that I cry out when I am lost for words
but that you groan within me with your crying (Romans 8: 26)

not that I have plans for you
but that you beckon me to walk with you
towards the future (Mark 1: 17)

not that I fathom you
but that you grasp me in my deepest secret (1 Corinthians 13: 12)

not that I speak of you with great wisdom,
but that you live in me and express yourself in your own way (2 Corinthians 4: 10)

not that I keep you tight under lock and key
but that I am a sponge in your ocean-bed (335)

not that I love you
with all my heart and all my strength
but that you love me
with all your heart and all your strength (John 13: 1)

For how could I seek you, call you, love you …
if you did not seek me, call me and love me first?
Thankful silence is my final word,
the best way I know to find you. ❧

BENJAMÍN GONZÁLEZ BUELTA, SJ *(p. 5)*

Christianity is a revealed religion. It is the religion of the revelation of God to humans. But, before we proceed, it is important for us to be certain that we understand well what «religion» is. The Cambridge Dictionary on line says that:

> Religion is the belief in and worship of a god or gods, or any such system of belief and worship.

The word religion comes from «re-linking», meaning that which links, that which makes a connection —the relationship of the human being with something, or with the One who is not human but rather transcendent, supernatural. It is, therefore, a mysterious human linkage with something that, although greater than —and neither controllable nor dominated by— humans, shows itself, manifests itself, reveals itself to them.

There are people who don't have, and don't intend to have, any religion. They don't believe in the existence of anything beyond that which we humans can see and hear with our own eyes and ears, and touch with our hands. But many others do have the experience of faith. They don't believe that all things end at the point where they can no longer be seen, heard and touched. They believe that there is something —or better said— someone, a person, who is above us, at our side and inside us, and who speaks to us. They are, therefore, religious people, that is, people who have a religion. Among the many religions in the world, Christianity is one of those with the greatest number of followers.

Many people are very religious, but not Christian. They believe in God, but not the God of Christianity. They live their faith in a different way from us. We certainly should dialogue with them, and there is much we can learn by doing so. The learning could be mutual, and mutually enriching. But for that to happen we need to know well our religion, which is Christianity.

There is no better way to define Christianity than to say that it is the religion of the revelation of a God to men and women. The revelation of such a God was received by the men and women of Israel and then by many others. It continues to be received by us today, and is preserved in writing, in a book. Christianity is, therefore, a religion of revelation and of the book.

Other men and women came to God in other ways. But we Christians came through the experience of faith, thanks to the Revelation of God to a people, the people of Israel. From the midst of this people emerged a man —Jesus of Nazareth— in whom we recognize the Christ, or the Messiah of God. That's why our religion is called Christianity—because it finds in Christ the center of its identity.

This history is —and was— important because it helps humans perceive the Revelation of God happening in their midst. For us Christians, the conviction that God revealed God's self, and continues to do so in history, is fundamental. We don't need to remove ourselves from history to be able to hear God, meet God and receive God's revelation. On the contrary, it is in history, our history, that we can hear God's Word and understand what it means for us. Christian Revelation, is, therefore, historic revelation.

2

God: The Spoken Word in History

The fact that a God communicates with men and women, talking to them in the midst of history, is central to the Christian vision. That is why the people of Israel began to see that what happened in their history of captivity and liberation, in their struggle to settle themselves in a land, in their need for political organization —among other things— were not isolated occurrences, unconnected to each other. Neither were these things related only to the immediate moment. They carried a bigger meaning that demanded great attention, because God was personally present in them.

Thus the people of Israel understood what was written after God's revelation to Moses —that this revelation resulted later in their liberation from captivity in Egypt and in their journey toward the land of freedom. It referred to God's self-revelation in speaking to Moses about what was seen in the history of that beloved people, and about what God intended to do in that history: «I have observed the misery of my people who are in Egypt; I have heard their cry on account of their taskmasters. Indeed, I know their sufferings, and I have come down to deliver them from the Egyptians, and to bring them up out of that land to a good and broad land, a land flowing with milk and honey ... The cry of the Israelites has now come to me; I have also seen how the Egyptians oppress them.» (Exodus 3:7-9).

This is the story of a God who speaks, and hears what is happening in the world and in the heart and history of humankind. Nothing that happens to men and women, God's creatures, leaves God's heart unaffected. And when what is heard is the clamor of lamentation and despair of a people suffering under hard servitude, God speaks out. And what God speaks is the word of life and salvation, of ransom for this people under the darkness of oppression.

The man who heard this revelation—Moses—was to have his life transformed and receive a mission that, although divine, was to be lived out in the heart of history: «So come, I will send you to Pharaoh to bring my people, the Israelites, out of Egypt ... I will be with you ...» (Exodus 3:10,12).

Likewise, once far away from captivity and settled in the promised land, the people of Israel—not to forget it— repeated every day the revelation that this God had so powerfully brought to their history: «A wandering Aramean was my ancestor; he went down into Egypt and lived there as an alien, few in number, and there he became a great nation, mighty and populous. When the Egyptians treated us harshly and afflicted us, by imposing hard labor on us, we cried to the Lord, the God of our ancestors; the Lord heard our voice and saw our affliction, our toil, and our oppression. The Lord brought us out of Egypt with a mighty hand and an outstretched arm, with a terrifying display of power, and with signs and wonders; and he brought us into this place and gave us this land, a land flowing with milk and honey» (Dt. 26:5-9).

Humans are historic beings. Their fundamental characteristic is their capacity for relationship and communication with others. For this reason they only see and learn that which happens in history and at the heart of several relational processes in their lives: their relationship with the surrounding world, with other human beings, and with the self-revealed God.

The people of Israel had perceived that self-revealed God in the midst of history and not outside it. Some historical events conveyed more than what could be immediately perceived with eyes and ears. These events pointed to that which was beyond, that is, to a divine disposition and providence. The presence of God was felt by the people in occurrences such as war, victory and defeat, the crossing of the Red Sea, the liberation from Egypt and the exile. Or better said, where others saw only war, victory, defeat, accident, and fatality, the people of Israel saw the presence of their God in the midst of all these events.

We see, then, that God's revelation is a horizon where one can read history from a holistic perspective. For the people of Israel history does not proceed only from the laws of necessity. For them, as for all those who have faith, nothing happens by chance. All that happens is moved by a greater MEANING, which is God, whose footprints and signs are left at the center of this same history.

3
God: A Salvific Word in the Midst of History

To state that God is present in history and gives it significant meaning is to state, as well, that in the interest of coherence and fairness one has necessarily to be committed to history and to the struggle for justice, peace and freedom. That is because history, as the place of God's Revelation, offers us:

 – a past as a reference point for «remembering» and narrating;
 – a present for acting and transforming;
 – a future to hope for, when the new and always unpredictable will be welcome, and in them we will be able to «re-cognize» the Word of the One who comes to meet us, talk to us and question us.

Because it is closely tied to Salvation, Revelation sees all of history as a History of Salvation. Indeed, for the people of Israel, from their beginning, there were never two different histories, namely:

 – a chronological one, profane, measured by time, with day to day episodes, where facts succeed one another without major connections or meaning; and
 – a transcendent one, in which the meaning of salvation is mysteriously present and blended with smaller everyday facts.

There is only one history. It is the History of Salvation, the history of God's love that saves us, and of our response —a response that is always partial and wounded by sin. This is the history recorded in the Bible. First there was the experience of the people of Israel with their God, followed by the need and desire to put it all in writing. Today we run this course in reverse order, but with the same result. First we read the biblical text —but we read it already encumbered with our own life experience. Then we face the experience of the people of the Bible as a living lesson for us. And we will thus interpret, with the help of the Bible, all that God has been doing in our lives that keeps on «saving» us —that is, liberating us from what prevents us from coming closer to God.

All this shows us that at the dawn of the Revelation to the people of Israel, the men and women who heard the Word of God were captivated by it, spoke of it, and identified their God as the Word —the Word that breaks the silence and speaks. The first experience with the biblical God is that of God as the Word —not of God as a mute idol, but as a living God who speaks. But if God speaks it is because there is a listener, a human being, man or woman, who has listened, who does listen and who speaks of what has been heard. The starting point for speaking of God in the Judeo-Christian perspective is, therefore, the human being.

4

Speaking of God = Speaking of the Human Being

It follows, therefore, that Theology and Anthropology are inseparable. Speaking of God necessarily implies speaking of the human being and vice-versa. Karl Rahner, the great theologian already quoted here, says that in the Christian Revelation the human being is both subject and object. This means that to a large extent the human being is a product of what he or she is not. It further means that the human being cannot come into being by himself or herself. The human being cannot make himself or herself exist. Another must give him or her being and existence, and he or she must receive it from this other. Otherness —the other— is, therefore, the fundamental basis of human experience. Human beings can obtain their self understanding only from the perspective of the other.

In his or her trajectory in search of self-understanding and self-realization, the human being becomes aware of his or her limits and also of his or her greatness. The human being discovers that he or she is a self-conscious being (conscious, that is, of his or her own limitations, and thus of his or her humanity) and is therefore capable of surpassing and of transcending himself or herself. In other words, the human being is as biological, mortal and vulnerable as all other beings, and at the same time is no less irreducible to anything or any living being in the universe. The human being is a finite being who is also, inseparably, a being of infinite horizons.

The human being receives freely from the other all this finitude closely related to infinitude and eternity, having done nothing to deserve it or elicit it. The human being is, therefore, a «posterior» being, a being who comes afterward. Human beings came after the Other who created them, after the creation of other things, so that upon being created and coming into the world, they found other creatures already on the face of the earth. Yet, the transcendental experience that constitutes the human being—an experience that reveals the «unutterable»—comes from a fundamental «anterior» disposition to a responsible freedom.

The human being is free. In other words, at the same time that he or she is free to say YES, he or she is also free to flee, to turn away from being, and to say NO. The transcendental or ultimate freedom of the human being is mediated by reality —or, better said, by corporality, by history, by time, by space— an all-encompassing dimension mediated by what is contingent and provisional. Such a dimension is provided by the Creator God, who nevertheless is only revealed in, or by, that which is not God.

The Revelation comes about in the midst of this mysterious dynamism. It is the mystery of salvation, a salvation that points to the primordial originality of the human being. Nonetheless it is a salvation that only appears as inserted into history, an insertion that is indispensable (not optional) to the human being. In this sense there are not two histories, but only one: the history of salvation (which may also be a history of perdition, following the human being's desire for freedom).

Men and women, as beings, are referred to as a mystery. In other words, they are beings under a mysterious alien control. That means that they are patients even when they are agents, unknown even to themselves. Salvation is, therefore, something that comes from God, from the Transcendent, and yet can be experienced by the human being, within his or her limitations. This experience takes place when a Word is heard that comes from another.

Because it is so fundamental for understanding the human being, this notion passes as a definition of itself: the human being is a HEARER of the WORD. If God reveals and speaks of God's self, pronouncing God's name and showing God's face, the human being is a hearer of this Word, of this God who expresses God's self in a Word —a Word that addresses the finitude of the human being regarding vocation, call, and transformation. It is the efficient Word, the Word that is the fountain of Life, the Word that says what it does and does what it says.

Therefore, for the people of Israel, the densest modality of their Covenant with God is found in God's act of speaking to them through God's men and women (I Sam.2:27; Lev. 16:29 and 24:27; Is. 6:8; Jer. 1:9). This is an experience that penetrates the totality of the human being, who understands himself or herself as a «hearer» submissive to the divine Word , and also as the earthly mouth of Yahweh.

The history of the biblical people and their God will be, therefore, defined by this Word of God, the Word that is the real God. The diverse literary expressions that form the polyphonic fabric of biblical text testifies to the variety of angles through which the biblical God understands and reveals God's self as the Word.

In *prophetic accounts* one can find the word of God occurring in the words of humans. The Word of God reveals the actions of God, and the inspired actions of human beings are lived out divine words. God is therefore the voice inside the voice of the prophet. God's Word takes over the prophet, doing through and in him or her what is said by the Word, and causing the prophet to do only what is said.

God's Word also has a strict relation with the cosmos. The creative word of Yahweh is a constitutive element of nature in its origin and activity (Is. 40:26; Jr. 37:6; Sl 147:15). The cosmos is, then, a source of revelation, a place of encounter with that Word of God, which never ceases its communication with the human being.

The Word of God is a prescriptive word as well, linked to ethics and the law. God proceeds ethically and would like God's creatures to do likewise. Yahweh's Word is divine Law and a point of reference for living the Covenant and listening to the prophets. As oral and written Word, the Law is like a pedagogy that enables the people to live in fellowship and in synchrony with their God, and at the same time to live out their freedom.

At the end of the first century of the Christian Era, the author of the Letter to the Hebrews would refer to this understanding of God as Word and say: «Long ago God spoke to our ancestors in many and various ways by the prophets, but in these last days God has spoken to us by a Son» (Heb. 1:1-2a). Jesus of Nazareth, whom the first Christian community recognized and proclaimed as the Son of God —and indeed as God— would also be recognized as the Word of God. This Word, after speaking in history through mouthpieces, signs and powerful gestures, assumed flesh and journeyed into the world —a Word made into one of us in the incarnation, life, death and resurrection of a human being like us.

5

God: The Word Made Flesh

The history of Salvation as narrated in the Bible by the people of Israel is, for us Christians, centered in the story of Jesus Christ. In him, history turns on its hinges and encompasses the whole arch of time. Christian faith proclaims that, in the fullness of time, Jesus will fulfill the promise announced in God's covenant with the people of Israel. Likewise it proclaims that this Covenant will never be revoked, and will be fully consummated in the ultimate fullness of history, when God will be all in all. Jesus Christ is the event that, transcending time, transfigures historical time and makes it intelligible in the light of God's Revelation. This time moves through several great stages. People will slowly discover the contours of God's face and God's profile through the following stages:

a) *The stage of the promise and covenant:* This is the stage in which God promises to be the God of the people, and Israel promises to be the people of God. God seals the faithfulness of the promise by making an explicit Covenant with the people in Sinai, after having freed them from their captivity in Egypt. This covenant throws light on the time in which the people of Israel are living, and gives them a perspective from which to understand all that has come before —the creation, the flood, Noah and Abraham. It will also help the people understand what will come after the covenant is sealed and established —the long wandering in the desert, the conquest of the land, the comings and goings of the people regarding faithfulness and unfaithfulness. The main characters in this first great stage of the history of salvation are several: Abraham, the father of faith and the model for a relationship with God; Moses, the liberator of the people, intimate with God, who receives from God's hands the code of the Covenant (the decalogue); the prophets, spiritual leaders of the people who interpret events in the light of the Revelation, always leaving the door open to the future. All of them are simply mouthpieces of God, who is the great character in this history, the self-revealing God in the concrete, in the incarnate, and in the lived-out history of the people's struggle and suffering, as well as in their faithfulness and sin.

b) *The stage of achievement and fulfillment:* In the fulness of time, after the people of Israel had passed through all the vicissitudes described above, and matured in their relationship with God, «God sent his Son, born of a woman» (Gal. 4.4). The achievement and the fulfillment of the Covenant's promise came to pass in Jesus Christ, born of Mary. He is the fulfillment of the promise. He is the Covenant made flesh, the key to the understanding of all that has come before, and all that will come after his return. We believe that after the Revelation in Jesus Christ there will be no other fundamental moment of Revelation with a radically new interpretation in relation to the one given in him and by him. Nothing that will happen before the consummation of human history will surpass the revelation of God in Jesus Christ, but all will need to be understood in its light. Jesus

Christ is God's own beloved Son who comes as the crown of the long prophetic preparation in the Old Testament. The New Testament presents him as the fullness of God's presence in the world. In the visibility and flesh of Jesus, the invisibility and transcendence of the God that «no one ever saw» is manifested. And so it is that one can only know the Father through and in the Son. Revelation arrives at its plenitude.

c) *The stage of consummation*: This stage adds nothing to what has already been revealed in Jesus Christ, but unveils and shows in total transparency all that was revealed in him. Revelation then, as a process, reaches its completion. The veil is not only partially lifted, as has been the case until now. What happens now is the full unveiling. The mystery «un-veils» itself in all its glory. Although there is an unavoidable continuity between historic revelation and the revelation of glory, there is also a discontinuity —in the form, in the surpassing of the transitoriness and fragility of the flesh, in the victory over death, and in the overriding of the dimensions of time and space with dimensions beyond time and space. Individually, each man and each woman who comes into this world will go through this stage at the moment of his or her death. However, the whole of creation waits collectively for this stage, when all things will be taken over by God's Spirit, and God will be all in all. Then creation will be fully capable of acknowledging the total sovereignty of Christ, and history will be filled and moved by the presence of the Spirit of God, who continually renews all things.

A Deeply Loving and Faithful God

1

Present Everywhere

You herald yourself in speech:
and emerge in silence.

You show your love in the gift of life:
and accomplish your self-surrender in the gift of your death.

You are dazzling in the prodigy of the day:
you enthrall us in the mystery of the night.

The holiest ones are the summit of your creation:
and the most iniquitous, the pinnacle of your fidelity.

The oppressed are the expression of your liberating power:
and of your patience and respect, those who oppress them.

You are the untiring artist in all that is beautiful:
strong, still presence in all that is malformed.

Geniuses tell of your boundless possibilities:
the broken of your probing questions, posed in solidarity.

You show your masterpiece only when all of history is run:
but even now you can illuminate the fullness of the ephemeral instant.

You call us without end from the horizon:
you imbue us with your presence at every twist in the path.

I will never capture you in the greed of perfection:
but your light and future already flow beyond my limits.

BENJAMÍN GONZÁLEZ BUELTA, SJ *(p. 42)*

From very early on, the people of Israel had understood their identity as one of a close relationship with the love of their God. The prayer with which the pious Israelite expressed his or her fundamental profession of faith already had a starting point in the love of this God. This would make possible the knowledge, the love and the perpetuity of the Law.

God's love opens the ears of the people and each one of their children, who repeat several times during the day: «Hear, O Israel: The LORD is our God, the Lord alone. You shall love the LORD your God with all your heart, and with all your soul, and with all your might» (Deut. 6:4-5). The God of Israel is a God who loves and wants to be loved with the full humanity of the human being. This is a God who not only can be feared, but also loved —which is something that had never been affirmed, before Deuteronomy.

This love is expressed by a person's total commitment, as invoked in the threefold expression: «with all your heart, with all your soul, and with all your might». In many other passages we find this love required, affirmed and reaffirmed —at times in a twofold rather than a threefold expression: «with all your heart, with all your soul» (Deut. 10:12; 30:6).

In still other passages of this book —a book that is fundamental for understanding the experience of the people of God— we find other words than *love* to express the relationship of the people with their God. They are «seek the LORD your God» (4:29); «serve the LORD your God (10:12); «observe these statutes and ordinances» (26:16); «return to the LORD» (30:2); «turn to the LORD (30:10). The biblical writer evokes with these different verbs the infinite concrete forms that love for God and also God's love —not only for the chosen people but for all those God cares for— can and must assume.

God's love is dynamic, radical, and perpetually in motion. God's followers are brought inside this infinite and irreversible movement. This love is not something that is acquired once and for all, but rather something one has always to look for, live out, listen to and obey. Something to which one must return if any distancing occurs. This requires one's whole heart, being, soul, and strength, leaving out no aspect of a person's life as less insistently or less strongly called.

If one thing can be said of the people of Israel —not forgetting for even a moment that they are the people of the Law— it is that they are the people of love. It is this love that will shape the life of the people, their way of being and their life project. Love of God will be the criterion by which the stature of each person and of the whole people will be measured.

2

God: Deepest Love and Patient Fidelity

In the beginning of their history the people of Israel did not have a very clear notion of their God in accordance with what we today call monotheism. Not yet understood as universal, God, the God of the people of Israel was the God of their ancestors (Deut. 26:5 ff). Monotheism had not yet arrived in the full meaning of the term. What prevailed was a monolatry—the people worshiped their God and only their God, among all the gods of neighboring peoples (Judg 11:17-24). The Lord was the God of Israel, because God had chosen Israel as God's people. God, therefore, was freely committed to the people of Israel, and vice-versa.

Once that first stage—of a newly liberated people in process of organization—had run its course, God came closer to the human being. This closeness is synonymous with a proposal, a pact, a liaison, a Covenant. Rather than the very superficial relationship based on rituals unrelated to practice, this is the inauguration of a relationship between the people and Yahweh that is much closer, and more personal and moral.

Faithfulness is the image of the relationship between the people and their God. Israel appears and is understood in this stage as the spouse of Yahweh. Yahweh is the spouse of Israel (Hos.2:14ff)—a faithful spouse who demands faithfulness, and is «jealous» when Israel worships other gods. Faithfulness is an essentially human attitude, and different from the incomprehensible rituals of the previous stage of religious existence. The fact that faithfulness is at the center of the experience during this stage reveals that Yahweh is no longer interested in superficial rituals, but rather in the heart of the human being (Am. 5:21). Morality expresses this faithfulness, which speaks through the deepest profundity of the human heart. Religion that is merely ritual is condemned. Also condemned is any ritual that fails to reach the human heart. The desert—a place of encounter and of coming back to the first love of youth—appears to be a time of faithfulness without ritual (Am. 5:21; Isa.1:9-17) and of contempt for a ritualism without soul and without justice.

The Decalogue emerges as the code of the Covenant. If Israel fulfills the commandments, God will fulfill God's part and protect Israel forever. The result is a historical posture: Israel must fulfill just one part of the Covenant (the commandments). Yahweh will take care of the rest. Israel will attend to morality, and Yahweh will attend to history and to Providence.

Every historical problem must, therefore, result in a moral renewal in Israel (Os. 7:8-11; Isa. 31:1ff). There will be two possible sins, as denounced by the prophets: unfaithfulness, or idolatry —the worship of other gods, and self-sufficiency, or the pretense of controlling events instead of trusting God's Providence.

The sacred and the divine appear here as moral and historical providence. God provides historical events according to the moral conduct of the elected people. The experience of God, which had been expressed in superficial rituals, now approaches the center of human existence—the heart. This implies progress in God's closeness to the human being. A new identity appears between religion and historical undertaking, as related to the notion of Covenant. The central discovery in this experience is that of the human being as God's collaborator, even if indirectly, in a design which will play out in History—a discovery that will need some refining. The definitive Christian Revelation will recapitulate all this in Christ, the faithful witness par excellence, who ransoms the totality of history with his incarnation, life, death and resurrection, inaugurating a new creation and being all in all.

The model for the people's leader should be the one who «loves the Lord» as the just and wise King Solomon did (1 Kings 3:3). In several passages of the Old Testament we find different metaphors for the love of the Lord, symbolizing how God's presence is more intensely revealed (Ps. 119:97, 165: «Oh, how I love your law!»; or the words that 1 Chr. 29:3 puts in the mouth of King David: «... I have a treasure of my own of gold and silver, and because of my devotion to the house of my God I give it to the house of my God»).

The Psalms are dotted with exclamations of this intense love by which the psalmist worships and invokes his God with several expressions of affection and praise, such as «my Strength», «my Song», «my Rock», «my Shield» etc.

Yet, all this experience of loving and being loved —which characterizes the way of the people of Israel— and all the undeniable and exclusive requirements of this love, will have been seen from very early times not only as affective and sensitive. There is a very concrete and real dimension in this love of God, which will require practice as demonstration of faithfulness to God. It is the practice of justice and right for all, especially for those who are most deprived of strength, voice and opportunity: the orphan, the poor, the widow, the stranger.

It is this way of loving God that the book of Leviticus will be concerned with in describing the Laws of Holiness —namely, the set of precepts that have as a common denominator the sanctity of God. This sanctity must transpire in all acts and circumstances of the life of a people consecrated (*qadosh*) to the holy (*qadosh*) God, as summarized in the precept: «You shall love your neighbor as yourself» (Lev. 19:18). The *ethos* of loving God above all things arises as a primordial requirement revealed in the face of the other, the neighbor, in relation to whom the people must practice this freely given love.

3

The Person of Jesus and The Following of Jesus: The Demand for Unconditional Love

‍

The commandment to «love your neighbor as yourself» (Lev. 19:18), combined with the commandment «You shall love the LORD your God with all your heart, and with all your soul, and with all your might» (Deut.6:5), will once again be taken up by Jesus to express what is essential in Moses' Law (Mt.22:37-39).

49

Revealing the God of Abraham, Isaac and Jacob, as his Father who demands unconditional love, Jesus proposes to his disciples something similar. The Sermon on the Mount (Mt. 5:43-47) —the Magna Carta of the project of the Kingdom of God— provides some new nuances on the appropriate and specific way of loving that the disciples must possess and witness.

The appropriate shape that Jesus gives to his teaching about love is unique. He not only interprets the Old Testament as do the learned and wise men of his time, but goes beyond that. He says something new based solely on his own authority (see Mk.1:22, 27 ff; Mt 5:21-22, 27): «You have heard that it was said to those of ancient times… But I say to you…». This is a word beside or beyond what «was said to those of ancient times…» by none other than God.

The «but I say to you» of Jesus can be understood as the definitive word of God. Unlike the prophets who dot their discourses with explicit references to the God of Israel in order to be very clear in whose name they speak —«Thus says the Lord» or «Word of Yahweh»— Jesus does not distinguish his word from the word of God. On the contrary, he understands himself to be —and is understood to be— the mouthpiece of God, indeed the real voice of God.

What is thus proposed to the Christian is active conduct: to endure and to be compliant in all things, and to actively and dynamically love every human being, including the evildoers. The principle (vv. 43-44) is to go beyond loving one's neighbor as required in the Old Testament, as *was said to those of ancient times*.

Here the mention of the enemy denotes a new antithesis (v. 44): «love your enemies».

But what kind of love is this? Certainly it is nothing like a spontaneous affection based on affinity, which would be impossible in such a case. The Greek word for this kind of love, the verb *agapan*, shows that it derives from a wish that is not compelled by the self-restraint that one must exercise in the case of enemies. Furthermore, one has to avoid a purely psychological limitation, because Christian love —charity— must be lived out as active goodness, conducive to beneficial and concrete results.

This teaching, thanks to the general word «enemy», includes any situation in which a Christian is mistreated or even subjected to death because of his or her faith. The subsequent antagonism (v. 46) between the «brother» and the «enemy» confirms that the enemy is neither a personal adversary within the religious community, nor the enemy of the nation in a military or political sense, but the persecutor of the faith, the enemy of the messianic community formed by the first Christians.

The motivation reiterated by the evangelist to sustain such love and its requirements is sought outside the world of God's creatures. The motivation capable of supporting such conduct is the imitation of God, and the desire to comport oneself as a child of God. According to the Gospel of Matthew, for Jesus of Nazareth one becomes a child of God the moment he or she begins to practice love for one's enemies as an imitation of this God, who shares grace and benefits with all human beings without exception. The «proof» that one is a child of God is found in faithfulness and obedience. Conformity with the Divine will expresses itself in Judaic ethics as imitation of divine conduct, directly in line with the conviction that the human being is the image of God.

A Christian should go beyond the conduct that requires loving one's neighbor *as oneself,* beyond the justice of the scribes and pharisees. He or she must do more than is required in the human categories mentioned, in comparison, by the evangelist. God in person, as the sovereign example, calls the Christian to a conduct that perpetually surpasses all limits: «Be perfect, therefore, as your heavenly Father is perfect» (v. 48).

Jesus, the Son of God, pushes his disciples to unsuspected limits. He doesn't simply propose an art of living in this world, but a positive obligation, a ministry of universal love. In this he goes far beyond the duty to forgive —although he includes it. His requirement to love one's enemies goes further, rejecting what remains of condescension in the act of forgiveness, even affirming forgetfulness in order to think about nothing except one's own generous gift, without resentment or hidden intentions.

It is simply an act of love, without any strategic intent to either keep a utilitarian peace at the service of church policies, or to use benevolence as publicity to attract converts. It is, doubtlessly, a love more divine than human. It would not be accessible to human beings without the courage to believe in the first commandment, *to love God above all things,* and the willingness to suffer «the loss of all things» in order to «gain Christ» (Phil. 3:8) and to attain —with him, by him and in him— a resemblance to the divine.

In his proposal to his disciples, Jesus invites them neither to recognize nor to impose limits when the issue is love. It is an invitation to «love above all things», because this is the way God loves.

The person of Jesus, the perfect synthesis of the human and the divine, will be the reference point that enables the disciples to understand that such love is not impossible for human beings inhabited by the Spirit of God. At the end of the Gospel of John, the One who is one step from Passion will say, as a testament to his dear ones: «I give you a new commandment, that you love one another. Just as I have loved you, you also should love one another. By this everyone will know that you are my disciples, if you have love for one another» (Jo. 13:34-35).

4

The God of Jesus Christ as a Condition for the Possibility of Love
⁓

Biblical revelation sees, in the human encounter with the one and only God, the Unconditional and historically revealed God as the foundation of the universal standard of *ethos.* Christian faith affirms the encounter with this God in Jesus Christ as the experience of a radical sense of existence, a basic theonomy of *personal* liberty and responsibility, indeed an experiential embedding of the person in the Unconditioned One who guarantees to him or her both personal liberty and limits.

The term used for this love of God is *ágape,* usually translated as love. Here we have a conception of love not adequately expressed by the verbs and nouns most frequently used to that effect in the Greek language, such as *eros, filia, storgé.* In *agape/*love the emphasis lies in a disinterested generosity —with the possibility of joy and satisfaction deriving only from its practice—and in a disposition for outreach in the direction of the other. Otherness incapable of desecration is the starting point of this self-giving, which has its roots in a self-giving God as the real gift. This self-revealing God is perceived and adored as the real love —as expressed with blinding clarity in the First Letter of John: «Whoever does not love does not know God, for God is love» (1 John 4:8).

Therefore the condition for the possibility of loving God above all things is found in God's own being. This God, who demands to be loved above everything and above all, is the God who, before everything, loves creation and humankind unconditionally.

The New Testament texts proclaim this truth with exceedingly emotional exclamations: «For God so loved the world that he gave his only Son, so that everyone who believes in him may not perish but may have eternal life» (Jn. 3:16); «If God is for us, who is against us? He who did not withhold his own Son, but gave him up for all of us, will he not with him also give us everything else?… Who will separate us from the love of Christ?… in all these things we are more than conquerors through him who loved us… nor anything else in all creation, will be able to separate us from the love of God in Christ Jesus our Lord» (Rom. 8:31-39).

That is why the First Letter of John states: «We love because he first loved us» (1 John 4:19). And loved us without restriction, without conditions. Indeed the loving dynamic into which this God takes us must be free from any kind of restriction or condition. It cannot be subservient to any other imperative or priority. It is and remains above all things.

It is true that the thoughts, words and works of human beings often hold no trace of faithfulness to the Revelation of the God —*ágape* in Jesus of Nazareth, which radicalizes and clarifies the revelation of the God of Abraham, Isaac and Jacob. But this does not mean that the light that shines on a life surrounded by the love of God will be extinguished. This is the same light that, according to the prologue to the Gospel of John, shines in the darkness «and the darkness did not overcome it» (Jn 1:5).

This light, which shone from all eternity, turned itself into the Word that was heard and obeyed in historical time, as expressed in the first commandment of the Old Testament: «Hear, O Israel: The LORD is our God, the LORD alone. You shall love the LORD your God with all your heart, and with all your soul, and with all your might» (Deut.6:4-5).

A Vulnerable and Compassionate God

Forgiveness Without Conditions

You festoon us with forgiveness.
You don't ask us to haggle with you
over punishments or deals.
«Your sin is forgiven.
Do not sin any more.
Go and live without fear.
And don't lug around the dead body of the past
on shoulders that are free».

You do not ask for security
on the unpayable debt,
of having turned against you.
You offer us a new life
no need to labour
overcome by anguish,
paying off the interest
of an infinite account.

You forgive us wholeheartedly.
You are not a God
who apportions percentages of love.
«To this one seventy five
and to this one only twenty three».
We do what we do,
we are sons and daughters, one hundred percent.

Your pardon is for everyone.
Not only do you carry the lost sheep
on your shoulder,
but the wolf too,
stained with sheep's blood.

And you always forgive.
You leap up to welcome us
on the road of return,
seventy times seven,
neither turning your face from us
nor rationing out your words,
for your repeated running away.

And with forgiveness you grant us joy.
You do not want us chewing over
our broken past,
in some corner of the house
like a wounded animal,
but celebrating the feast
with all our brothers and sisters,
dressed in party-best and perfumed,
entering into your joy.

We ask you in the Our Father
«Forgive us as we forgive».
Today we ask you still more:
teach us to forgive others
and ourselves
as you forgive us.

BENJAMÍN GONZÁLEZ BUELTA, SJ *(p.50)*

The face of God shown in Biblical revelation is far from that of a God who is distant from human suffering, far from that of a God whose transcendent womb is unmoved and unaffected by what happens in creation. Such a God, unattainable in absolute transcendence and keeping an unbridgeable distance from human beings, would be more compatible with the several varieties of theism than with the God of revelation.

From very early times, but especially during the transition between the 17th and 18th centuries with the philosopher Leibnitz, the question of the compatibility of God's existence with the presence of evil in the world was intensely considered. In his reflection on the creation Leibnitz tackled the problem of divine justice, and especially the issue of how sin, evil and suffering are possible in a world created by God. For him this was the problem of «theodicy», a term he crafted. His answer was complex, covering many pages of *Théodicé*, the only one of his philosophical books to be published during his life-time. In summary, his argument was that evil is a necessary and inevitable consequence of God's decision to create the best of all possible worlds. No matter how bad we may think things are in this world, we must conclude that they would be much worse in any other world.

Three-hundred years before Christianity, and much before the Greeks, the myths and ancestral religions were already facing the impossible equation of the presence of the gods and the reality of evil in the world. In classic antiquity, Epicure posed the intricate question: «Either God wants to eliminate evil from the world, but cannot do so; or God can but does not want to do so; or God neither can nor wants to do so; or God can and wants to eliminate it. If God wants to and cannot, God is impotent; if God can and does not want to, God doesn't love us; if God neither wants to nor can, then God is not only unkind but also impotent; if God can and wants to —and this is the only alternative remaining for God— then where is evil coming from, and why doesn't God eliminate it once and for all?»

In the early Middle Ages Boethius, in his *The Consolation of Philosophy*, said something similar: «If God exists where does evil come from? But if God doesn't exist, where does good come from?» In the 20th Century, in 1947, the great French writer Albert Camus published his book *The Plague*. There, in the middle of a narrative about a city attacked by rats, where people are dying like flies, an atheist doctor and a priest confront each other about the meaning of all that. While the priest firmly stands on his faith in God despite that hell in which children are attacked by evil, the doctor and narrator, Rieux, hurls strong invectives against God, saying that it would be better if God did not exist, because if God exists and allows all that, then God is a true monster. Rieux does not find the faith's answer, although he constantly hears his friend Tarron questioning whether it is possible to be a saint without God. And Camus says through his character that he will refuse until death to love this creation in which children are tortured, and that he has no intention of lifting his gaze to heaven, where God is silent.

The Bible proposes a different route for this difficult question. According to the Sacred Scriptures, beyond human pain and suffering is the compassion of God, as well as God's creative and productive life-force. The world is not evil. It could not be, because it is God's creation. But God creates the world and human beings in freedom, and in freedom God respects the choices they make. They are free to choose life or of death, thus introducing disorder and chaos into creation.

The biblical God is not an absolute anonymity, not a general conception. This God is rather a living and personal God, indeed a God with a name and identity, whose face is shown and whose name is revealed. This God relates outward, in personally structured relationships under God's own name. God's behavior is, therefore, inseparable from the revelation of God's being.

The biblical God, moreover, is the God of Israel, the God of the people, the God of our parents, the God of Abraham, Isaac and Jacob, the God of human beings, the God of the community, and the God of the Covenant. God is not an autocratic monarch, a solitary power, but rather the God who affirms existence as the community God. God's outward works and absolute transcendence correspond to the logic of what God is in God's self. God's action truly follows God's way of being, in both in the Old and New Testaments. God is revealed to the people of Israel and in Jesus Christ as the God of the eternal Covenant, the social God.

The biblical God of the Old Testament walks with God's people and suffers with them. God goes into the exile with God's people, thus revealing God's self as compassionate and present even in the midst of the most absolute disgrace. The Shekinah of God goes into exile with the people and assumes their suffering, helping them perceive that in the deepest of their pain and abandonment they are not abandoned —because that same God who was capable of liberating them from Egypt and of giving them a new land was also capable of giving a world to the human being. And this God is the creator of all that exists.

In the New Testament the cross is specific to Christianity. Although the resurrection is the final word of the Father on the death of Jesus, there would be no resurrection by avoiding the cross. In the *kenosis* of the Son who annihilates himself and divests himself of his divine prerogatives (assuming the figure of a servant and being obedient until his death on the cross), in the pain of the Father who suffers the death of his only and beloved Son, in the suffocation of the Spirit by the power of darkness —in these God does not appreciate human suffering from the safety of heaven. Rather God suffers, «compassionating» in the Passion of the Son with the misfortune and destiny of God's creatures.

God's compassion is even deeper than the deepest of human suffering. Even before human compassion, there was divine compassion. The God of Revelation is the One who cares for human beings, loving them from God's own deepest suffering. This has always been the way of the God of Israel. Christian faith proclaims that in Jesus Christ God reaches the pinnacle of compassion, of deeply loving, of becoming impotent through the unconditional surrender of God's self. God goes deep into in the misery of history, suffers inside it, and thus transforms it —turning love into the last word on the human adventure.

Compassionate until the end, God accompanies the human being in pain, thus transforming human life. True compassion is a creative compassion, which transforms all those under its influence into creators as well. Similarly, the only true humans are those who fully enter into the workings of creation, a place not only of beauty and goodness but also of suffering and evil. Only those who run the risk of suffering in their works, while carrying them out in the midst of their pain, are worthy of calling themselves human.

That is God's way of being, acting and creating. God runs risks, wishing us to be scandalously as well as dangerously free. God stands in solidarity with our freedom and assumes our destiny. Indeed compassion is part of God's deepest identity and an expansive expression of creative force that presupposes intensely and freely creative action.

At the dawn of humankind there was no mark of death on the forehead of the murderer Cain, but rather a mark of life. God does not imitate the murderer, who eradicates otherness, but on the contrary, traces the mark of blessing on the foreheads of both victim and executioner. In response to the pain and death of God's Son on the cross, God does not annihilate the murderous humankind. Instead, God resolves that this world will continue and arrive at its plenitude, by continually re-creating it in unending and compassionate love.

As for the characteristics of the personality, sociability and compassion of God, no doubt the Trinitarian concept is more appropriate than either monotheism or the Greek categories. The creative and loving compassion of God can only be imagined when the infinite value of persons is assumed. True passion and true love will consist in loving others in their difference, in their personal identity, in helping them to fully be what they are, that is, creators of themselves.

As proposed to human beings, this attitude can only be theologically interpreted from a Trinitarian perspective. God's life is the matrix for their being, their life, and their action. To love is to enhance the being of the other. In line with that, the Father fully delivers his whole being to the Son without transforming Son into Father, thereby blurring the distinction. Father and Son give themselves to each other, sharing between them their infinite and eternal divinity in an expression of the love partaken in the Spirit, who is love itself. Human persons are images of divine persons. For this reason they are called to mutually love, condole, and help one another in an expression of creative compassion, while offering and sharing existence.

The personal aspect of the Trinitarian understanding of God tells us that God exists as Father, as Son and as Holy Spirit. These are proper nouns and not general concepts. This is the enunciation of a relationship within God. And this enunciation is the inspiring and existential matrix of human beings as relational beings. The infinite and inalienable value of the human person is not centered in the individual, and much less in reason merely understood as the informative and intellectual *therefore* that confirms the *cogito* of Descartes: «I think, therefore I am». Although indeed a thinking being, the human person is, before that, a person in relationship. In living out the relationship, the human person is a being infinitely loved by the Creator, and consequently endowed with individual, unique and inalienable rights.

Faith in the Trinitarian God thus motivates the discourse on and commitment to the affirmation and promotion of human rights, which has been central in the most recent history of humankind. What secular society advocates through international agencies for the protection of human rights, Christianity proclaims based solely on faith in a God who is, from eternity, a person in an inexhaustible relationship of love and compassion.

The Trinitarian God, a community in God's own being, also incorporates the dimensions of unity, plurality and differentiation. This God is, in God's self, a communion. In the beginning there was no loneliness of a solitary deity inhabiting indomitable heights. In the beginning there was communion. We are children of this communion, not of loneliness. God is the seminal and transcendent communion, the foundation of the identity and ways of human beings.

This conception of God is important for understanding the human being as a social being who is not centered only in him or herself, but in a commitment to the society in which he or she lives. The worship of the Trinitarian God takes place in community, in sociability, in participation. Social commitment, therefore, finds its roots at the center of faith in the God one believes in.

The God of revelation, in revealing God's self both as a person and as a community of persons equally reveals God's self as a womb of mercy and compassionate love, who is not alien to the most obscure pain of the least significant human being. On the contrary, this God is completely distinct from the impassive and apathetic Greek gods, and is not indifferent to anything that happens to the human being. This God is deeply compassionate. The Trinity's center is the Passion of Christ, the Easter Mystery. Therefore God is not alien to pain. God is the One who, having inwardly assumed pain, redeems it while giving it meaning.

The Father of Jesus Christ is not the God of the gentiles, the God of the philosophers, who have no answer to human despair other than a distant and tragic silence. On the contrary, this is the God who has personally assumed the suffering and mortality of creatures, and, therefore is a vulnerable and compassionate God—vulnerable not because of imperfection or need, but because of love.

Such a compassionate God is permanently identified with the victims and sufferers of this world. Although God's infinite love saves both executioners and victims, it is in their tortured, massacred, painful bodies that God can be found, and in no other place. As long as there is in the world one single person suffering injustice, being mistreated and crushed by aggressive and blind violence, one can find there the God, Father of Our Lord Jesus Christ, who did not spare God's own Son, but surrendered him for all.

The writer Elie Wiesel, an Auschwitz survivor, quotes in his book *Night* a pungent and moving story that helps corroborate what we say about divine compassion. It is based on the rabbinic theology of the self-humiliation of God in God's death, and it strengthens what we just affirmed:

> The SS hung two Jewish men and a youth in front of all the interns of the camp. The men died quickly, but the agony of the youth lasted for half an hour. «Where is God? Where is he?», asked a man behind me. When after a long time the youth still hung in torment in the noose, I heard the man cry again: «Where is God now?» And I heard a voice within me answer: «Where is he? He is here—he is hanging there on the gallows».

Christian theologians such as J. Moltmann, E. Jüngel, B. Forte and J. Sobrino wrote comments and reflections on this and other terrifying experiences of Elie Wiesel and many other Holocaust survivors. This enabled them to continue to think of God after the genocide which shook the world in the mid-20th Century. Their reflections follow a line that in other circumstances would be considered blasphemous. Nor could there be any other Christian answer to the question provoked by such infamous torment. To speak here of an impassive God would certainly convert God into a demon. To speak here of an absolute God would run the risk of converting God into no more than a destroyer. To speak here of an unconcerned God would condemn human beings to abandonment and indifference.

Only God's compassion can provide a meaningful answer to this anguished questioning from the human spirit. God's compassionating —that compassion of God which penetrates, assumes and redeems human suffering— is the only opening for dealing with the enigma of evil in the world, for living and suffering it without falling into despair. The vulnerable and compassionate God is the only God who saves. And saves by compassion. Saves by vulnerability. For if God weren't vulnerable and didn't suffer, God would be incapable of love and wouldn't be called love, as God so beautifully is by the First Letter of John («God is love» 1 John 4:1).

Those who believe in this God must live out the adventure of love and charity in all its varieties until the end, including through martyrdom. Because irrespective of the angle from which we look at God, we will find there only love and compassion. «Thus God is at the same time the lover —the Father, beloved —the Son, love itself —the Holy Spirit».

A Father God with a Maternal Womb

1

A Maternal God

The woman's maternity
so close to life's mystery
is privileged language
for penetrating the action
of God in our history,
bringing up new life
from our abyss and darkness.

There is a *time of gestation*.
«For a long time I have held my peace,
I have kept still and restrained myself (Isa. 42;14).
There are no signs of new life,
only the silence of God
before the triumph of injustice.
In the womb of history
a new liberated life
is being formed in silence,
according to the rhythms
of human processes.
For the superficial gaze
God does nothing,
The people is abandoned (Isa. 54:1).

When the *hour of the delivery arrives*,
«I will cry out like a woman in labor,
I will gasp and pant» (Isa. 42:14).
As if God indeed
were in labor,
assuming the cry of pain,
the lacerating suffering
accompanying the birthing
of the future kingdom,

opening the way
among personal resistence
and the controls of laws and masters.

With a *new life*
comes joy and feast.
«Sing, O barren one
who did not bear;
Burst into song and shout,
you who have not been in labor» (Isa. 54:1).
God cares for the fragile life.
It is a time of affection and caresses.
«As a mother comforts her child,
so I will comfort you» (Isa. 66:13).
The newly born future,
carried by the hands of God (Isa. 42:6),
grows up slowly
until it acquires full stature.
«In righteousness you shall be established;
you shall be far from oppression» (Isa. 54:14).

We are tempted to shout
in the middle of history's night:
«The Lord has forsaken me» (Isa. 49:14).
Beholding the love
of the unfathomable mothers
who are faithful to their children
even if the hard life
separates and confuses them,
we come near so as to understand
the faithfulness of God
to the life born from your hands.
«Can a woman forget her nursing child,
or show no compassion for the child of her womb?
Even these may forget,
yet I will not forget you» (Isa. 49:15).

If mothers create the future,
expressing divine maternity,
this abyssal mystery of life,
reaches its ecstasy in Mary,
the virgin and poor young woman of Nazareth,
the mother of the always young word
under the shadow of the Spirit.

Benjamín González Buelta, SJ

Nowadays, history is essentially the story of humankind's emancipation from authoritarian and patriarchal conceptions of life and society. If this were true and unavoidable, would it mean that God's paternity is an anachronistic idea? Would it be an empty gesture to speak of God as Father to human beings for whom paternity has no value and is associated with negative ideas?

Ours is an era in which battles are fought for several types of emancipation. On the one hand there are huge masses of oppressed people who have become aware of the acute injustice of their condition. The poor see no improvement in their lives on the horizon. The same is true for the victims of racism and dictatorship, as well as for women, who are still treated as inferior beings. Many young people have the impression that nothing is there for them, and even church members complain that their voices are never heard by their leaders. The protests from these groups are often so utopian that they can result only in disappointment and frustration.

On the other hand there are those whose main concern is to defend the cohesion of society and the validity of traditional norms. Their idea is that all opposition to authoritarianism opens the door to anarchy, making it necessary to give serious consideration to their concern about the growing lassitude in the heart of society and its consequent disintegration. Yet conservative and neo-conservative movements of both left and right ideological orthodoxy do not manage either to stop the wave of desire for emancipation or to reduce the resentment of their adherents. Those who consider emancipation a panacea and those who see it as a fatal disease are both heading into a blind alley. It is time for us to ask ourselves if true emancipation was not what the Prodigal Son discovered when he returned to his father's home, a place of enduring love where the prevailing order was neither domination nor anarchic freedom.

2

A Society with Fatherless Children

While studies on the consequences of inadequate maternal care abound, not enough has been said about the devastating effects of the lack of a paternal figure, which produces as many victims. According to current psychological research, some of the infirmities that have plagued recent generations of children —such as anorexia, bulimia and toxic dependence— can be directly linked to the absence of paternal influence. Similarly, the absence of a positive masculine figure linked to strong paternity can be found at the root of phenomena such as neonazism and other forms of youth delinquency. From a psychoanalytic point of view, to be deprived of a father is tantamount to being deprived of a backbone.

Ours is a generation of all kinds of emancipation as well as a generation of earthly and heavenly fatherless children. The lack of a paternal figure opened the way in more advanced societies for the growth of the sects. The absence of a father in a basic institution such as the family reverberates in political structure with the growth of totalitarian systems and «charismatic figures», which symbolically point to a search for paternal attributes such as those of judge, protector, etc.

The demise of the ideology of the father is visible in the great uncertainty about the future and the past which characterizes our age. The debilitation of the three commanding paternal metaphors (labor, personal lineage, and roots in a specific place) has ruptured the support for our existential anxieties, expressed in questions such as «where did we come from» and «where are we going?»

The cultural legacy of Freud and other modern thinkers makes many interesting contributions to the hermeneutics of human development and social functioning. For instance, they confirm the truth that wherever there is no father there is no sibling relationship, but rather a struggle for supremacy leading to expulsions from a center which must be occupied in exclusive ways. The sibling also tries to eliminate by force something (such as an inheritance) of which he or she could be otherwise deprived. This idea is already discussed in texts of the gospels where sons and brothers compete with the father or stepfather for the inheritance (see the parables of the prodigal son and the wicked vineyard tenants). In these stories the image of greedy paternity preventing the well-being of children conflicts with Jesus's attempts to reveal and communicate something completely different.

While this modern critique of paternity as oppressive authority may be pertinent and positive, it is certainly true that the disappearance of the father leaves an irreparable emptiness in the minds and hearts of our contemporaries. In a sense this can be verified by the fact that today's fathers no longer know how to be teachers. They don't know what to teach or to whom. This brings us back to the gospel text in which Jesus himself «de-identified» earthly paternity from the paternity of God: «And call no one your father on earth, for you have one Father —the one in heaven. Nor are you to be called instructors, for you have one instructor, the Messiah» (Mt. 23:8-10).

The surpassing or even elimination of today's Father can only be, in theological terms, a recovery of the more authentic meaning of God's fatherhood —beyond all its referential symbolic and liturgical debilities— in an anti-authoritarian way, and above all in the context of the general uneasiness of a culture in conflict with its deepest foundations.

3

A Father God in the Bible

Father —the word evokes biblical images, including those in dreams: the man at the door of the tent, the murmur of women, children and animals, the king in a royal place, and also the affectionate gaze, the blessing, the silvery hair, the frail body, the death bed. In patriarchal times the chief of the clan —father of a multitude of children— was an obligatory reference in the narrative of the discovery of his God. Before the contours of God's image amongst the people became clear, the God of Israel was referred to as a father or paternal figure.

In spite the various hypotheses to explain and interpret these namings, designations such as «the God of Abraham», augmented by «your father Abraham», «Abraham, Isaac and Jacob», appear in patriarchal narratives that literarily highlight the predominance of family over tribe and state. The relationship of the human being with God is, therefore, seen from the perspective of the father-son analogy.

Patriarchal accounts do, undeniably, have a familiar character. The God of Genesis 12 is a God who accompanies and protects the family, or a prototype of the human family —humankind. The divine promise and blessing point to the future while rescuing the past of the great human family. Abraham—Isaac—

Jacob—12 children—12 tribes: this is how Israel understood its own history—as a succession of «fathers». Thus, even the names of the twelve tribes are interpreted from the standpoint of the numerous progeny. And the memory of the people is preserved in line with what «our ancestors have told us» (Psalms 78:3-7).

However, not all that is said in the Old Testament about the central importance of the human father refers directly to God as Father. The gaze of faith in the Old Testament that allows one to see and follow the path of the revelation of God as Father, is conditioned by the gaze in the New Testament—by Jesus's invocation of «Our Father», by the sovereign title of Jesus himself as «God's Son», and by the divine filiation of Christians. This is where the essential parts of New Testament theology, christology and anthropology, are articulated. One cannot look only in the Old Testament for the model and the objective basis, par excellence, of the «religion of the Father». The anthropomorphism of God as Father is not a primary theme in Old Testament theology, but rather an accessory to it. The naming of God as Father is explored in the Old Testament with extreme caution.

The representation of God's physical fatherhood, in the mythological sense, is not found in the Old Testament. This is due to the Old Testament's conception of God as «pure» and «transcendent»: Yahweh has neither wife nor specific sex, and of course, in *stricto sensu*, no children. Unlike so many other gods in the areas surrounding Israel, the category of sexuality does not apply to Yahweh.

In some Old Testament passages God becomes father «by adoption», especially in accounts from the royal davidic period (2 Samuel 7:14). The most direct enunciation of this is found in Psalms 2:7 where a descendant of David proclaims: «I will tell of the decree of the LORD: He said to me, "You are my son; today I have begotten you"».

But that refers to a begetting by protocol, not to a natural one. The decadent exaltation of royal ideology will result in the erosion of the idea of the king as mediator between God and human beings, as well as of its paternal-filial reference to God. The people of Israel will understand themselves as Yahweh's children adopted through free and sovereign election (see Hos. 11:1; Jer. 3:19 ff). In any case it is not a natural link. Psalm 109:13 and Proverbs 3:12 confirm that Israel's experience of God is above that of the natural human father. In their understanding of God as a human father, God's paternal essence is received as a benefit. And as for the attributes of a father, God's being can be interpreted from the angle of majesty (the One who punishes and inspires fear) and from the angle of kindness (the One who loves and corrects).

During the time of severe tribulation in Egypt, the deutero-Isaiah beseeches Yahweh for freedom and sovereignty, evoking images of the potter and the father (Isaiah 45:9-11):

> *Woe to you who strive with your maker,*
> *earthen vessels with the potter!*
> *Does the clay say to the one who fashions it,*
> *«What are you making?» or*
> *«Your work has no handles?»*
> *Woe to the one who says to a father,*
> *«What are you begetting?» or to a woman,*
> *«With what are you in labor?»*
> *Thus says [Yahweh],*
> *The Holy One of Israel, and its maker:*
> *Will you question me about my children, or*
> *Command me concerning the work of my hands?*

Isaiah 63:15 ff:
> *Look down from heaven and see,*
> *from your holy and glorious habitation.*
> *Where are your zeal and your might?*
> *The yearning of your heart and your compassion?*
> *They are withheld from me.*
> *For you are our father,*
> *Though Abraham does not know us*
> *And Israel does not acknowledge us;*
> *You, [Yahweh], are our father;*
> *Our Redeemer from of old is your name.*

And so the People express their belief that their destiny depends on the mercy of Yahweh. Nothing greater was said about the Father in the Old Testament, and the comparison in no way diminishes the unique character of the divine Father. Yet we find nothing to express Yahweh's inner essence, which in its vital force and generative potency is stronger than that of the human father. Therefore the most powerful guiding thread in God's revelation as Father in the Old Testament is certainly God's condition as Creator.

God the Creator

The creative Word of Yahweh is the constitutive element of nature in its origin and activity (Isa. 40:26; Job 37:6; Ps. 147:15). And the cosmos is the source of God's revelation. God is, therefore, the One who creates existence, the One who calls things to come into being from where they are not. And God does so by God's Word. God speaks and it is done, from nothing. Only God is God, as will be repeated many times in the Bible, meaning that only God is capable of creating from nothing the cosmos and all that exists (Isa. 40:25-30; Job 38).

As God creates, God brings order to the created. God's Word provides structure to chaos. At the same time the Bible reminds us that the Creator dialogues with humans, thus showing immense respect for them. All this happens with an absolute lack of violence, in a kind of fundamental gentleness which later, in the New Testament, will be the sustaining basis of the Sermon on the Mount —when the perfection of the Father will be proclaimed (Mt. 5).

In this creation —which happens in time, «in the beginning»— the biblical account doesn't dream of contrasting God's eternity with the eternity of the created world. Only God is the origin and beginning of all that exists. The world comes afterwards, although it is not possible to establish chronological dates for this posteriority of the created. This «beginning», this «origin without origin», which only finds its ineffable source in the divine Fatherhood, is incomprehensible without an «end». Yet this end, without which the world would lose its dynamism, is radically unknown to us. That it is unknown prevents us from searching for it among the phenomena of this world. This end is not available to the scientist. It is also unknown to the Son, who leaves this secret with the Father (Mt. 24:36).

The effort by Christian Theology in recent years to bend on the issue of the Creation signals a conscious awareness on the part of Christians that the ecological question involves much more than a new subject to be taken up by theology. It is an issue that affects the future of the human-nature-God relationship. In other words, it affects the central concept of God in Christianity: the Father God, author of life, creator and savior.

The mandate of «having dominion» over the earth —words that the book of Genesis (1:28) puts in the mouth of the Creator God, addressing the man who was just formed from clay and animated with the divine breath of life—has gone through many interpretations throughout Christian tradition. One of them —and perhaps the most prevailing among Christians— tended to interpret the divine order as defined by an arrogant rule over nature by human beings, in the name of the Creator. Yet this is simply one of many tendencies that, far from presenting an anthropocentric and predatory vision of nature, propose a contemplative view of the world —seeing it both as a human habitat to be loved and respected, and as a medium of God's self revelation.

Even so, this tendency continues to present problems as Christianity confronts current ecological challenges. Accusations and mistrust linger regarding the interpretation of the mandate in Genesis as that of absolute and limitless primacy of the human being over nature, carrying with it serious consequences: the concept of an unequivocally individualistic human being allied to an omnipotent economic and technological determinism; the vision of a human being separate from nature, who sees it as an enemy to be conquered and destroyed with impunity in the name of an equivocal progress; and the human struggle for life transmuted into a menacing instinct to kill directed against all other forms of life.

Theologically the consequences are no less serious. To opt for such a tendency and to assume such an interpretation is to introduce an irreparable split in the idea of creation by separating the human being from the cosmos. It deprives the Christian life from its own theology and spirituality —from the notion prevalent among the ancient people of the cosmos as an epiphany, as the manifestation of a mystery that demands reverence and respect from those who approach it. This is a filial attitude that must be one of the governing principles of Christians towards the whole world.

It is an unavoidable imperative for Christians today to reacquire a contemplative and ecstatic gaze in order to see in the world, in reality, in all living beings, the common mark of God's creatures —the divine creation as a home for God and the human being.

In this manner Christian theology opens the way for theocentrism —or the centrality of the God who is the Creator Father as well as the Spirit and life that inhabits both the human being and the cosmos— in place of the anthropocentrism that has characterized it, proposing either the crisis of paternity or the elimination of the paternal figure. In this perspective, person and planet obtain equal rights. The human being is no more important than other beings, but is a humble co-citizen of a community of living beings —a community which preceded human beings as they emerged from the Creator's hands.

Christian theology should, therefore, surmount the ecological crisis by returning to the question of the God of the Judeo-Christian revelation, of whom the human creature is image. This is a God who reveals God's self not through domination, but by surrendering prerogatives in humility towards the creation —in order to reveal God's self in it, to dwell in it, to know and to be known. To know the creation does not mean to dominate it, to reduce it, to transform it into an instrument, but rather to remain modestly and wonderfully schooled by that love that respects it, and to enter into relationship with it.

From this standpoint, the world will be lucid and transparent through the divine presence, unfolding its mysteries and charms to a human gaze purified of all instrumentalist voracity and made capable of contemplation and adoration. In it human beings will be called to discover their place, which is partnership and communion with the totality of the cosmos. The starting point for Christian anthropology is the indisputable fact of the earthliness of the human being and the human species. The second chapter of the book of Genesis deals with this theme. It introduces the first man very clearly to the reader, calling him —and the human species he symbolizes— the «earthling», «the earthly one» (*adam, adamá*). Humankind and all other animal species are made from earth. From earth they come and on earth they depend for breathing, nutrition and survival.

Yet, as they discover and come to understand themselves as «earthly beings», Adam and his lineage also perceive that the earth does not belong to them. Its rhythms and secrets are impenetrable to them. Only slowly and deliberately is the key to some of its mysteries delivered to them. In a certain way the earth «resists» the human being, which is why some cultures and traditions proclaim it as sacred and, with filial affection, venerate it as a Mother pregnant with life. If, in biblical experience, no explicit trace of an earthly cult can be found, neither can any trace be found there of a «cult» proclaiming human supremacy as a creature. The author of creation, according to the Bible, is God. And the whole creation carries the capacity to generate life. This capacity is, in itself, sacred and undeniable because ultimately the Giver of life par excellence is always the Spirit of God. To be created is already and inseparably to be a participant in the true being and true life of God. The world and humans are fully co-participants in this life. And if something else is given to the human being, it is nothing more than the added responsibility as the guardian and protector of created life —the administrator, in the midst of the cosmos, of the God of life and of the work of God's hands (Gen. 1:28-31).

Although the creation is worthy of reverence as the place and home of life, it is not considered in Christianity to be a harmonic greatness reconciled with itself. It is, indeed, a divided, conflicted and suffering greatness, traversed and «subdued» by evil. All creatures partake of this condition and together groan and wait for liberation (Rom.8:19-22). Christianity, for its part, proclaims that only passing through the messianic filter of the new creation, inaugurated with the incarnation, life, death and resurrection of Jesus Christ, would justify the claim, at the end, that the world is grace.

The habitation of God in the still enslaved creation is, therefore, a gift, although a wounded one, exposed and vulnerable to the aggression introduced and established by the disorder of evil. According to Christian theology, it is not a distraction from ethical matters, carried out for leisure and aesthetic tranquility, for humans to behold the cosmos and to enter into relationship with it. It is rather the awakening of a basic ethical concern —that of giving (or giving back) to the dispossessed and exploited man and woman a place which is theirs, the cosmos. This restitution is something to which the human being has a right granted by none other than God. It takes the form of restoration of bread to the hungry, solace to the homeless, and water to the thirsty, among other things —amounting to nothing more than the restitution of a piece of the cosmos to those who were deprived of it. This gesture of ethical restitution is, according to Christian logic, the fundamental redemptive and salvific action as well as the Eschatological Judge's measuring rod for judgement at the end of times (Mt. 25:31-47).

As the place of ethics and moral action, the creation is also the place of the pitiable, the downtrodden, and the vulnerable. If something is to be restituted, this something is a symptom of the loss, privation and suffering of the assaulted. This loss carves in the cosmos the sign of *pathos*. The inordinate use of nature's resources brings suffering as much to the human being as to nature itself, giving rise to a clamoring for a greater measure of solidarity, sharing and reconciliation. Besides being —almost by definition— the place of experience, the cosmos is also the place of ethical questioning and of a receptivity that tests and is tested, as well as the space of passion and compassion. If Christianity's starting point is the fundamental truth that God's Word became flesh and came into the world, where it lives and finds its dwelling, the world itself witnesses this deeply loving presence which, upon entering creation, devotes itself fully to the act of experiencing and knowing its creatures. Self-exposed by «being in the world», and self-deprived of divine prerogatives (Phil.2:5-9), God assumes in the vulnerable flesh of Jesus of Nazareth the consequences of the beautiful —although often suffering— interaction with the cosmos and with things. The suffering caused by the uncontrollable calamities that descend upon nature is not ours only but God's as well. It is indeed undeserved suffering, which highlights the realm of the unexplainable, and is experienced as painful.

The incarnation of the Word, for its part, refers back to the act of creation by the Father God out of nothing *(creation ex-nihil)* and to the origin of times. Some strands of contemporary theology —in direct dialogue with tendencies of Judaic thought— see in such an act the first gesture of the divestiture of God, who, in creating heaven and earth «alien to God's being, opens» a finite space in God. It is in this open space, «capable» of finitude, that the cosmos will appear, «capable» in itself of receiving God as a vivifying presence as well as a loving and salvific vulnerability. It is an ethical and emotional space, the primal point of fecund contractions, pregnant with life from the Creator Father God. However, according to biblical revelation, the cosmos is not guilty but is rather captive and submissive. Passively delivered to vanity, in the words of the Apostle Paul (Rom.8:17-31), it suffers the consequences of human sin. The source of its ill is, therefore, disgrace, not sin.

Thus nature —creation and daughter of the Father God— has not been corrupted, but simply wounded. And what is true of cosmic nature can also be redeemably true of human nature which, in its relation to the cosmos, is not substantially corrupted in its profoundest depth. Human nature continues to be potentially «capable» of goodness and reception of divine salvation. One cannot forget that the cosmos, an ethical and emotional space, the place of experience, of experiment and passion, is also the place of historical praxis. The Christian proposal is above all an offer to recover and rescue —to save— the meaning of the cosmos and the human being, aiming at the manifestation of a new creation. This newness, which the Christian is called by the Gospel (and inspired by the Holy Spirit) to bring into creation and history, is nothing more than the original design of the Father God Creator and Savior, and necessarily includes this world and the struggle to transform it.

Christian theology humbly begins with the faith that the Father God wishes to make effective right now, in creation and history, the salvation that will reach its consummation in «trans-history». While eagerly waiting for that, the Christian is called to love with undivided heart this world, which God «so loved that he gave his only Son» (John 3:16, 17, 18) and upon which God poured, and always continues to pour, the New Spirit of life and sanctity. The «figure» and finality of the Human-God-Nature relationship is therefore love. A love, indeed, that is not only enraptured and devoted, but also effective and transforming. It is love that knows not only how to admire and behold, but also how to experience, struggle and suffer.

The Cosmos and human beings reciprocally carry in their being a common destiny. It is a destiny of salvation. As a bearer and means of salvation, the cosmos tells us today that whatever was created is saved, because it carries in its profoundest depth a vivifying presence of the Father God Creator and savior. The cosmos is thus our soteriological space, where we can experience and be experienced by the Spirit of God, who inhabits the very center of creation as a gift as well as a loving and redemptive vulnerability. On the other hand, the human being is responsible for the future of the cosmos. He or she is called not only to construct a history and a plan for his or her own growth and progress separately from the rest of creation, but also to care for and ensure the livelihood and absolute survival of all living beings, and all creation. The ecological questioning heard and heeded by theology could be helpful today in preventing the forgetfulness of this mutual fecundity and interpenetration of person and planet in loving compliance with a common Father Creator.

The new attention to the question and theme of Creation, in Christian thought, touches the core of the mystery that animates it and gives it consistency, a mystery that reveals itself, today as always, not as logical mystery but as mystery of salvation. The salvific desire of the Father God, who is at the beginning of everything that exists, is for the glory and joy of God to be manifest in the life of the creatures —among themselves and with God— a life in communion similar to the life, glory and joy of God's immanent being as Father, Son and Holy Spirit.

5

The Father with Maternal Womb

The Revelation of this Creator and Father God reached its fulness in Jesus Christ. This, for its part, will lead to the revelation of the feminine and the maternal in God. In recent years, indeed in recent decades, valuable articles and even books have been written on the subject. Also, in the 60's and 70's the feminist movement participated in anti-paternal and anti-authoritarian recriminations with an anti-masculine tone. The assassination of the father, in feminist reflection, is a «farewell to patriarchy». That mystifying institution attributed universal value to the male, failed to recognize any prejudice regarding the female, and systematically provided weight and space to the masculine throughout history and in hermeneutics. At the beginning of the century there was already a new hermeneutic of the feminine in the theological field, as well. Among its radical achievements was to place institutional-religious orders under a common accusation of guilt in imposing the equation «God is male, therefore the male is God».

«Beyond God the Father» is the meaningful title of the book in which, at the beginning of the 70's, Mary Daly declared the impossibility of a reconciliation between Christianity and anti-patriarchy, and the establishment of a new and diverse religious symbolism. Man erroneously identified himself, in the name of God, with the «father» assassinated by the model of feminism in reality and action.

Other, more fecund, avenues of feminist thinking are those giving critical attention to the Father symbol, pointing out the danger of parallelism between the concept of «boss» and the paternal name attributed to God from the Latin concept of *pater familias*, as well as the need to separate the two. The true meaning of God's paternity, according to the Judeo-Christian revelation, is a more fertile one based on the concepts of creaturely dependence and confidence in being strictly united and related.

Even masculine theology highlights, in the paternal concept of God, the meaning of God as both the source of a new life and its protector. In this sense, the God of Jesus Christ is *Abbá,* namely, the intimate God who is maternal in caring for God's children and in being attentive to humankind. With the maturation of feminine thought and the emergence of other tendencies, a deeper and more valuable effort prevailed —the restoration of the distinction between the man (male) and God, and the recovery of a filiation (a being in relationship) with the Father that was hidden and disguised in many iniquitous mediations. Both the mystical and monastic traditions of the last century promoted the pursuit of feminine identity and liberty in relation to a living God, discerned in the passion of an identifying endeavor with strong and exclusive feminine connotations. Christian feminine thought retrieves from the heart of tradition, and underscores especially in the figure of Mary, a status of «female daughter» of highest value. Not only is similarity with the Father established as the highest divine prerogative (namely, to be a giver of life), but the woman's subjectivity receives a strength and freedom unattainable in any other way.

Again, regarding the question of divine femininity-maternity raised by feminist thought, one finds still standing the urgency to recover the most authentic sense and meaning of God's paternity beyond the need for such a name as an obligatory symbolic and liturgical reference. The crisis of the «paternal order» is, therefore, linked to the crisis of masculinity. The latter, appropriately, received strength and identity from the symbolic attribution de-legitimated by the feminist reaction to anything it found negative in the androcentric tradition. With the war waged by femininity against the patriarchal tradition, the continuity of the transmission of masculine values, which was a foundation of male identity, became even less effective. Today's father suffers the consequences of the de-universalization of masculinity, which subverted established hierarchies. Feminism, as remarked by the French thinker Elizabeth Badinter, exposed the «naked emperor».

This point is made to exempt feminism from the current and inexact accusation of being solely responsible for the current crisis of masculinity. But in this context there was the denunciation of a dangerous and challenging aspect of feminine thought and action in confronting man: coming to see, analyze and express with exceptional lucidity his limits and deficiencies, and to find themselves superior in a different way from that of men in regard to women.

For man, to see woman as inferior was a theoretical and mental question, deepened to enable him to approach her without fear, while for the female to gaze at actual masculine «nudity», without a capacity for love and mercy, would make it impossible or difficult for her to think of herself at the man's side, and would therefore have a highly disorienting effect. The awakening of consciousness achieved by recent generations of women differentiates them profoundly from the foremothers, who «saw man as a God», and probably had fewer problems and a simpler life.

There is a nucleus of a legitimate theological basis for women's desire and struggle to be men's companions and to work side by side with them, rather than making of them inferior or lesser beings. We can say this because we believe that the divine being that created us, that redeems and sanctifies us, is not more identified with one gender than with the other. On the contrary, in transcending both genders God brings together men and women without eliminating the wealth of difference between them. We believe that there is a feminine as well as a masculine principle in our creation in the image of God, in our salvation made possible through the Incarnation, Passion and Resurrection of Jesus Christ, and in our new being molded by the Spirit of God. Nevertheless, the masculine principle has been much more broadly recognized. This makes even more important the fact that the feminine principle today is out of that hiding-place where it was kept throughout all the years of a Judeo-Christian tradition molded by a predominantly masculine patriarchal culture. It is time for us to rethink our faith in God. A faith in God that is identified only with masculine characteristics is incompatible with the Christian revelation and with the God of love revealed in the Bible, and most fully in the New Testament.

Our reflection is, therefore, based on the conviction that only an inclusive masculine and feminine image of God, integrating the fullness of humankind —masculine and feminine— as well as the cosmic reality, can adequately serve as a symbol of the divine. If the human being is the image of God (Gen. 1 & 2), then in examining our concept of the image (the human being) we see analogically the characteristics of the model (God). In the Judeo-Christian tradition, and even in today's so called western Christian civilization, this concept has been decidedly androcentric (cf. the tradition of the account of the creation in Gen. 2:18-24). In the narrative of the covenant, the divine partner (God, Jesus Christ) is represented by masculine elements, and the partner that is human and a sinner (Israel, the Church), by feminine elements. According to Saint Augustine, the woman can be considered God's image in her rational soul but not in her sexed body. On the other hand, for him the masculine gender itself symbolized the excellence of the divine image. In this type of body-soul dualism man is theomorphic. And God, the universal God of all peoples, becomes (although that may not have been the intention of the authors) andromorphic. According to this typology it is not difficult to see why God is always called king, judge, patriarch, husband, lord and father. Along with this notion of masculine supremacy comes the traditional notion that a woman can reach that level only when she loses her femininity, that is, when she renounces her sexual functions, thus transcending her gender and identity.

When this anthropology is applied to the image of God, one finds an abyss between humanity and femininity. A God thus conceived identifies God's self with only one gender. Although we find aspects in Scripture and theology that are predominantly masculine, we can also find some feminine and maternal characteristics in God. The feminine language and images that can be glimpsed in

Scripture allow us to see God's feminine characteristics. Thus we can find in God not only a strong Father but also a Mother who is compassionate, comforting, and protective, who shows not only strength but also creativity, balance and beauty. The God of Christianity is not a lonely dominating patriarch, isolated in heaven. God is a community of love among three persons (Father, Son and Holy Spirit) whose commonalities and particularities are not suppressed, but integrated, and whose life is an integral process of procreation and birth. In this divine community, the human community —made up of men and women— finds its similarity.

In both the Old and New Testaments one finds certain semantic «nuclei» that enhance our access to feminine reality in the divine mystery. One of the biblical expressions often used to that effect is *rachamim*. It describes clemency, God's mercy. Its root term is *rechen*, which means womb. As *rachamim*, it refers to that place in the woman's body where a child is conceived, nourished, protected, and where it grows and is then brought into the light. The word *rachamim* is, therefore, used to compare the love of God to that of a mother.

In Isaiah 49:15 God is compared to a mother: «Can a woman forget her nursing child, or show no compassion for the child of her womb? Even these may forget, yet I will not forget you.» In Jeremiah 31:20 the prophet refers to God's *rachamim*: «Is Ephraim my dear son? Is he the child I delight in? As often as I speak against him, I still remember him. Therefore I am deeply moved for him; I will surely have mercy on him.» Isaiah 42:14 suggests that God's sufferings for God's children are like birth pains: «For a long time I have held my peace, I have kept still and restrained myself; now I will cry out like a woman in labor, I will gasp and pant».

Thanks to the mysterious intimacy of motherhood, this unconquerable love is expressed in many different ways in the Hebrew Bible: as protection and salvation from different enemies and dangers, as forgiveness for a person's sins, and also as faithfulness in keeping promises and in nourishing hopes, in spite of the unfaithfulness of others (Hos. 14:15, Isa. 45:8-10; 55:7, Mic. 7:19, Dan.9:9). God's *chesed*, God's profound clemency and faithfulness to the people regardless of their unfaithfulness and sins, comes from God's maternal heart, God's *rachamim*. God will always be compassionate and infinitely loving (Isa. 14:1).

Israel's faith petitions this God as a mother's womb. It calls for and requests loving protection: «Look down from heaven and see, from your holy and glorious habitation. Where are your zeal and your might? The yearning of your heart and your compassion? They are withheld from me» (Isa. 63:15); «Has God for-gotten to be gracious? Has he in anger shut up his compassion?» (Ps. 77:9). Psalm 79:8-9 (a) mentions the «divine *rachamim*» as if they were the actual God: «Do not remember against us the iniquities of our ancestors; let your compas-sion come speedily to meet us, for we are brought very low. Help us, O God of our salvation, for the glory of your name».

All these texts lead us to question why this God, who is known and worshiped as a strong deliverer, invincible warrior and powerful Lord, cannot also be known as a loving and affectionate mother. These words from Scripture make us feel that it is possible to experience God in maternal ways.

The term *ruach* is evocative, as well. In the Hebrew Bible it means «wind», «spirit» or «breath of life». It is a feminine word. Sometimes in the Old Testament this wind is a pleasant breeze, on other occasions it is a strong wind (I Kings 19:11, Isa. 57:13, and others). Sometimes God sends the wind (Ezek. 1:4, Dan. 7:2), at other times God is in the wind, which is the breath and life of God (2 Sam. 22:16, Ps. 18:16, Isa. 11:15 etc.). *Ruach* is the Spirit of God and the presence of God, the giver and carrier of life.

In the account of the creation of the world (Gen. 1:2), when the *ruach* moves over the earth it evokes the presence of a Great Mother who brings the world into the light from her generous and loving womb. Paul Evdokimov, the great Russian Orthodox theologian, says this about woman: «She is under the sign of the Spirit, who, in the narrative of creation, broods and hatches the egg of the earth». This same Spirit appears as *ruach*, mother of life, and gives the breath of life to all that exists (Ezek. 36:37, 1 Sam. 10:6-10, 2 Kings 3:1ff). In another group of passages the *ruach* appears as God (Isa. 63:10-11, Ps. 51:13). These passages, being more recent, are the basis for what in the New Testament will be the Holy Spirit (Mk. 1:9-11 etc.), who was called, in many ancient texts, not comforter but comfortress.

There are other meaningful words in the Old Testament such as, for example, Wisdom (*hochma, sophia*), described in the Scriptures as a «daughter of God». With her, God creates and fulfills the work of giving life. In Proverbs 8:23-31 this same Wisdom, mediator of creation, is imagined as a mother who conveys wis-dom to her children.

The author of the Book of Wisdom portrays her as a feminine presence, God's mediator and a presence in the history of salvation. She was their companion and guide; she helped them through difficulties and dangers. She crossed the Red

Sea with them; «opened the mouths of the mute and gave voice to the tongues of infants» (Wisdom 10:21) so that they might worship Yahweh.

What is described is a «feminine type» of presence and activity. It is useful to compare the account of creation in the first chapters of Genesis with the description of the activity of Wisdom inside creation (Proverbs 7-8). In the one, God fashions «places» and creates forms of life. We watch God in action, making the world. God sees this from the outside, and is satisfied. This is a masculine image of conscious, visible and reasonable planning. In the passages of the book of Proverbs we see creation as a continuous process of «ordering» —shaping, inspiring, sustaining, and changing from inside. It is likewise a work of power, but from inside the domain of life, and can only be completely understood by someone who lives with Wisdom.

In the New Testament we don't find the same type of feminine images applied to God as are found in the Old Testament. Jesus, the Son of God, is, obviously, a man. He refers to God as Abba-Father, which is without doubt a masculine name. The Holy Spirit, the third person of the Trinity, is called *pneuma* in Greek. The gender of this word is neutral, neither masculine nor feminine. There is, however, a word used in the scriptures attributed to John that has strong roots in Christian tradition and refers to the mystery of God. This word is *agape*, which we translate as «love». «God is Love» (1 Jn 4:8-16). It is a meaningful word, not because its gender is feminine in Greek, but because of the deep reality it expresses. John's *agape* is God's love poured over the world. The loving relations that it initiates promote and encourage fellowship among people.

God's love for humankind, which flows from the Trinitarian economy, is the image and shape of God's deepest reality. Love thus mysteriously understood is inclusive. It does not exclude the poor and the least of the world. Trinitarian reciprocity is the matrix of inter-human reciprocity, the first and the last element of all that exists. In the same way that the Son and the Holy Spirit are a reference to a Beginning without beginning, an absolute Mystery, so too the Father, and thus also man and woman, come into being via a dynamism that transcends them and constitutes the mystery of the human being.

Each person in the Trinity shows a harmonization of feminine and masculine characteristics. The Trinity is a love community that revealed itself in feminine as much as in masculine ways.

Conclusion: I Believe in a God who is a Maternal Father

~

The disappearance of patriarchal structures represents a real revolution which affects the totality of human language about God. It is the deepest paradigmatic change in the history of Christian doctrine.

In relation to anthropology and the concept of God, the divine image is found as much in women as in men. If the God we believe in has characteristics and moods that apply to both masculine and feminine behavior, then from now on, in order to describe God, we will have to employ words, metaphors and images that are both masculine and feminine. If women no less than men are theomorphic, or made in the image of God, it is imperative that this God, of whom both are the image, be described or thought of not simply as andromorphic, but as anthropomorphic as well. We realize that we will have to deal with the poverty of human language and its limitations in expressing the majesty and ineffability of the divine. Meanwhile we will try to combine two symbols, two languages, and two metaphors—masculine and feminine—in our humble hope of achieving a better description of the divine.

A God Son with an Obedient Heart

1
Jesus

Jesus of Nazareth,
word without end,
in your little name,
infinite caress,
in your worker's hands,
forgiveness of the Father,
in streets without liturgy,
Almighty Lord,
in homeless sandals,
axle of history,
growing day by day,
brother with no borders,
in a reduced geography.

You are not a capital letter,
too big to fit
in the mouths of the littlest and the least,
but bread crumbled
between the fingers of the Father
for all simple folk.

You are ever
the water of life,
bottomless well
in the frayed knapsack
of the future seeker,
a blue lake
in the unsleeping hollow
of the pillow,
and a sea so immense
that it only fits

in a heart
which has no doors or windows.

In you everything has been said,
though for now, we drink in your mystery
sip by sip.

In you we all find our home,
but we only comprise your body,
name by name.

In you all is risen,
but we can only take on your future
death by death.

And today in each one of us
you will keep growing
till every name,
race, clay and creed,
achieve your stature. ❧

BENJAMÍN GONZÁLEZ BUELTA, SJ *(p. 78)*

For the New Testament and for the Christian faith, Jesus of Nazareth —whom the first communities recognized and proclaimed as the Christ of God— is not only someone who reveals God, but is also THE revealed God. Yet the course followed by this revelation and confession of faith is neither simple nor direct.

In the New Testament, for example, the word GOD is directly applied to Jesus Christ only seven times:

1 John 1:1. In the beginning was the Word, and the Word was with God, and the Word was God.
2 John 20:28. Thomas answered him, «My Lord and my God!»
3 Romans 9:4-5. They are Israelites, and to them belong the adoption, the glory, the covenants, the giving of the law, the worship, and the promises; to them belong the patriarchs, and from them, according to the flesh, comes the Messiah, who is over all, God blessed forever. Amen.

4 Titus 2:11-12. For the grace of God has appeared, bringing salvation to all, training us to renounce impiety and worldly passions, and in the present age to live lives that are self-controlled, upright, and godly, while we wait for the blessed hope and the manifestation of the glory of our great God and Savior, Jesus Christ.

5 1 John 5:20. And we know that the Son of God has come and has given us understanding so that we may know him who is true; and we are in him who is true, in his Son Jesus Christ. He is the true God and eternal life.

6 Hebrews 1:7-8. Of the angels he says, «He makes his angels winds, and his servants flames of fire.» But of the Son he says, «Your throne, O God, is forever and ever, and the righteous scepter is the scepter of your kingdom».

7 John 1:18. No one has ever seen God. It is God the only Son, who is close to the Father's heart, who has made him known.

In the last example, however, the word «God» does not appear in most manuscripts. It is therefore considered a problematic passage.

These confessions of faith, communicated through quiet and unquestioning affirmations, could be shocking when compared with certain texts of the Holy Scripture. Such explicit affirmations seem very distant from the New Testament texts that are so parsimonious and delicate in their pronouncements regarding the divinity of Jesus Christ. It is a serious and delicate topic, and requires a reflection equally serious and profound. What is in play is nothing less than the entire edifice of our faith and the concept of our salvation.

It is not only we who have such questions. Those who lived with Jesus and the generations that followed had them too. This problem was raised and solved by the New Testament theologians who, inspired by the Holy Spirit, gradually discovered who Jesus was and who was the God whom he called Father. Afterwards they wrote about his experience of faith in a God who reveals God's self as Father, Son and Holy Spirit, while being only one indivisible God.

Those who knew and lived with Jesus continually discovered his divinity in his humanity. To the extent that they kept experiencing a relationship with his humanity, with his fraternal and harmonious way of living, with his teachings full of love and authority, they further discovered in him the revelation of a different God. As they lived and related to each other they were deeply intrigued by this difference, until they arrived at a confession of faith affirming that the Jesus they had seen, heard, and touched with their own hands, was the Son of God and also God.

But even so, how is it possible to affirm that «Jesus Christ is God?»

Looking at the revelation of God in Jesus Christ in the New Testament, we find constantly in action a bipolarity, a fecund tension between two poles—*The Kingdom* and *the Abba (Father)*— today indissolubly linked in the person of Jesus. Jesus neither talks of himself nor preaches about himself. But he constantly talks about the Father, with whom he is in deep and ceaseless communion. And he talks of the Kingdom, a plan of his Father that he wants to bring about and make real. It is through this plan that human beings have access to the God of Jesus, to the God that he calls and teaches us to call Abba and Father.

While Jesus does not speak explicitly of himself as the Son of God, it is nevertheless true that those who wrote the gospels perceived, interpreted and registered his christological and divine intention. They perceived that something unique and different passed between this man and God that immediately made him both like and unlike other human beings.

2

The Christ of the Faith: Locus of a Tension

The question of the historicity of the figure of Jesus is of fundamental importance for Christology. But it concerns a historicity that begins with a believing and historically situated community.

Christology does not develop in a purely conceptual and speculative way. Thus, a positivist historical-critical method cannot by itself account for the whole complexity of the figure of Jesus of Nazareth and for his significance for Christian faith and theology. The effort by the Christian community to formulate its experienced relationship with Jesus Christ, in its own socio-culturally determined way, expresses the significance of the person and work of Jesus. At the same time it defines the Christian reality of the community. Between Jesus Christ and his witnesses there is an inseparability that bears on the directions that may be taken by faith in, and by later reflection upon, his person—which is the essence of Christology.

From this standpoint we can say that all revelation in the New Testament is pervaded by a dialectical tension between the «historical Jesus» and the «exalted Lord», which is perceived, believed and revealed by the mouth of witnesses as they confess their faith. The one who was «seen, heard, and touched by hands»

(1 John 1:1)—the historical figure of the son of Mary, the son of a carpenter, whose brothers and sisters were known among the people, who died on the cross—is inseparable from the one who manifested himself resurrected and glorious, with divine power and authority. Based on this tension, modern Christology conceived the identity of Christ as the object, par excellence, of Christian faith.

The *Christ of the faith*, therefore, according to contemporary theologians, is not a christological concept in opposition to the concept of the *historical Jesus*. Rather it includes the latter in its totality. The dynamic unity between the historical Jesus and the resurrected and exalted Lord at the right hand of the Father —this is the Christ of the faith, this is the One who was confessed by the mouth of witnesses «who saw and gave testimony»— is the central point of the Gospels and the whole New Testament.

The Gospels are not biographies. Neither is the New Testament in its totality a merely historical document. Based on authentic historical reality, the New Testament authors offer their interpretation by faith of the historical-transcendental facts that mark the life, death and resurrection of Jesus. To approach him is to approach the mystery of his person, of his figure, and to be questioned by the mystery at every historical and cultural moment experienced by humankind.

Because he is not merely one historical figure among others, Jesus Christ is a reference for all persons in all times and places. Because he is not simply a projection of earlier communities, and has historical solidity, through his real place in history Jesus Christ can help concretely each man and each woman in their spacial-temporal circumstances. The names and titles that the witnesses gave to this One whom they confessed as their Lord, can help us understand something about his complex and fascinating identity.

3

Some Titles that Help with the Recognition of Jesus Christ

The earliest witnesses needed to find names and titles to announce and proclaim the mysterious identity of this man, whom they had met one day and who had completely changed their lives. Although these titles are too numerous for us to analyze all of them in this section, we will highlight some that may help us as we try to improve our knowledge of the mystery of Jesus, which emerges from a fecund tension between history and interpretation.

1. *Jesus, the Messiah (= the Christ — Christós): Christus* is the Latin form of the Greek *Christós*. This word corresponds to the Hebrew *masiah* and refers to someone who has been solemnly anointed for an office. The hellenized form of the Hebraic word is *messiah*, which appears in the New Testament only twice, and only in the Gospel of John (1:41 and 4:25). In both instances it is translated, by the same evangelist, as *Christós*, and refers to Jesus of Nazareth. The decisive point to be emphasized about the word *Christós* in the New Testament is that its witnessing of Jesus of Nazareth is consciously «christological», in spite of its minor differences in detail from the expectant messianism of Judaism at the time. When Jesus is spoken of in the New Testament it is always as the Messiah-Christ. This means that throughout the New Testament messianism is no longer a matter of expectation, but of fulfillment. The Christ event is mentioned everywhere in the past tense. Of course the evangelist's gaze turns to the future as well, and sometimes with great intensity. But the One who is awaited as someone who will arrive is in reality someone who returns. He is not unknown. On the contrary, he is as well known by his people, who eagerly await him, as they are by him (Jn 10:14 —the passage of the Good Shepherd).

For the Christian faith, therefore, the name Jesus Christ embraces much more than the messiahship of a certain Jesus of Nazareth, in whose person God fulfilled the promises made to the people of Israel. In the New Testament the whole salvation that God had planned and brought to the world is linked to Jesus as the Christ. And if Christ —an honorific title— became a constitutive part of the name of Jesus, it was because it expressed the essential aspect of his historical appearance —the presupposition of his whole work as mediator of salvation. And this includes his obedient submission to the will of the God that he names as *Abbá* = Father. In this connection the «yes» of Jesus to his messianic vocation means for the *kerigma* of the early Christian communities the presupposition of his way to the cross, as well as of his resurrection and glorification. Jesus is not a triumphal messiah. Indeed, the most complete expression of his messiahship can be found in the so-called christological hymn, included by Paul in his letter to the Philippians (2:5ff), describing the way of Jesus as *kénosis*, humiliation and obedience until his exaltation at the right hand of God.

For the ecclesial community it will be of fundamental importance to perceive and follow the way lived out by Jesus of Nazareth in the earthly phase of his life, which is characterized as «emptying service». In this phase the community observes the attitudes, priorities, behavior, preaching and options of Jesus.

It perceives that these elements of his historical life have pragmatic value. «In order to recover the messiahship of Christ one has to return to Jesus of Nazareth. But then we will find an unexpected newness: Jesus is a crucified Messiah. This must be incorporated, as well, in the current understanding of the Messiah». And even if it is not a case of *literal imitation* but rather of a *creative pursuit which is new at every step*, the community feels itself led by the same Spirit that stimulated Jesus during his life: the spirit of service on behalf of life for all, beginning with the most marginalized. Even if the circumstances in which this discipleship takes place may be different and might be changing day by day.

The messiahship of Jesus Christ, by not being something that conforms to a present in which God's elected people have already received complete fulfillment of God's promise, reminds us that we must always be in tension with the future, the direction from where it will come. This is because the Christian faith proclaims that this Messiah, so eagerly expected by the people, has not only already come but will come again in glory. Christian existence, therefore, from the standpoint of the messiahship of Jesus, is called to be a constant announcement of the good news that the One who has come will come again, will recognize his people and will be recognized by them. Meanwhile we must position ourselves to follow him, in obedience and humility as well as in constant service to the dispossessed.

2. *Jesus, the Lord (Kýrios)*: The Greek word connotes a lordship that enjoys legality and represents a recognized authority. The designation of Jesus as *Kýrios* corresponds to the treatment given to the earthly Jesus. It possibly refers to the title *rabbi* (master), implying the recognition of his person as a superior, and the disposition to obey him (Mt. 7:21, 29ff, Lk. 6:46). This sets Jesus above human and religious institutions such as the Sabbath, and means that the words of the earthly Jesus have unquestionable authority for the community, even after his death and resurrection. The invocation by faith of *kýrios*—which primarily originated in the pre-pauline Hellenistic community—indicates that the New Testament community is submissive to its Lord (Phil. 2:11). As the exalted *kýrios*, Jesus Christ rules over all of humankind and the whole cosmos. Before him all living beings in the cosmos will bend their knees, since honoring him is the same as honoring the real Father God, at whose right hand he sits (Eph.1:20, 1 Pet. 3:22). Thus Jesus receives the same titles as God (1 Tim. 6:15, Dan. 2:47). At the time of the New Testament the relationship of Jesus Christ with the Father God was already being thought about —albeit not in a profound and well-developed reflection. The

New Testament would be the basis upon which the Church's Trinitarian doctrine would later be articulated.

Yet, the proclamation of Jesus as Lord has a particularity that makes his lordship different from all others and completes the profile of this Lord, who is the center of Christian faith from its origins up to our days. The *lordship* of Jesus Christ is inseparable from his *service*. His lordship reveals itself in humble service, without triumphalism. The exalted Lord is inseparably the Servant of God. And it is due to his condition as servant that he can be proclaimed as Lord. The concept of Servant —as presented, for example, in Mark 10:44— undoubtedly reflects Isaiah 53, in that it carries with it the *'ebed ywhw*, the center of interest of the songs of the servant of God, which according to an ancient tradition was applied to Jesus. This theme pervades all the Synoptic Gospels, although often it is not expressed with the word servant *(doulós, paîs)*, but with *hyiós* (= *son*) (Mk 1:11ff = baptism; Mk 9:7 = transfiguration).

In John we find no reference to Jesus as servant *(paîs or doulós)*, but only as son *(hyiós)*. Yet, depending on the circumstances in the Gospel, the thematic motif of the servant also appears (John 13:4ff —*the feet washing, humble slave work, done by Jesus on the eve of his passion*). Furthermore, in John we find Jesus portrayed as the Lamb of God *(to arnion tou theou)*, a clear reference to the Servant of Isaiah 53, who «like a lamb that is led to the slaughter... so he did not open his mouth» (cf. vv. 4-7).

4

Jesus, the Lamb of God who Takes Away the Sin of the World
⟡

The basic word used by the Deutero Isaiah to designate the Servant of Yahweh in the great prophecy of expiation in chapter 53:7 —and later applied to Jesus by the Christian community— is the Hebrew *rahél* (whose root is *rhl*), which means, precisely, *adult female sheep*. It appears four times in the Old Testament: Gen. 31:38, 32:14, Song 6:6, Isa. 53:7. In the last passage the Prophet says of the Servant: «*like a sheep (rahél) that before its shearers is silent, so he did not open his mouth*».

Also in the Old Testament, the word lamb *(kebes)* is used primarily in the priestly document of Leviticus and by Ezekiel in the context of worship. The lamb, as sacrificial victim, is an important part of Israelite worship. In the temple lambs are offered as burnt sacrifice and victim (Lev. 9:3, Num. 15:5), and as purifying expiation for the people or for individual persons (Lev. 14:10-11). The sacrifice of the lamb is also a central element in the liturgy celebrating the Jewish Passover, memorializing the exodus from Egypt.

What is surprising and original in the text of Isaiah 53:7 is that, for the first time in the Old Testament, one finds the transposition of such a function from sacrificial animal to person. Here Yahweh's servant, patient and suffering, is compared to a lamb dragged to the slaughter, to a ewe that is silent before her shearers and does not open her mouth. This text will be fundamental for the theology of the New Testament, where Acts 8:32 cites the Deutero Isaiah and applies that prophetic passage to the «Gospel of Jesus», to the heart of the good news that Philip volunteers to teach to the eunuch in the court of the Candace.

«Now there was an Ethiopian eunuch, a court official of the Candace, queen of the Ethiopians, in charge of her entire treasure. He had come to Jerusalem to worship and was returning home; seated in his chariot, he was reading the prophet Isaiah. Then the Spirit said to Philip, "Go over to this chariot and join it". So Philip ran up to it and heard him reading the prophet Isaiah. He asked, "Do you understand what you are reading?" He replied, "How can I, unless someone guides me?" And he invited Philip to get in and sit beside him. Now the passage of the scripture that he was reading was this:

> "Like a sheep he was led to the slaughter,
> and like a lamb silent before its shearer,
> so he does not open his mouth.
> In his humiliation justice was denied him.
> Who can describe his generation?
> For his life is taken away from the earth".

The eunuch asked Philip, "About whom, may I ask you, does the prophet say this, about himself or about someone else?" Then Phillip began to speak, and starting with this scripture, he proclaimed to him the good news about Jesus» (Isa. 53:32-35).

The New Testament, on the other hand, also follows the reference of the ancient culture, in which sheep belong to the category of minor cattle and are often mentioned in the plural, as a herd or flock. In the New Testament, the Greek term to designate the suckling lamb of the ewe, the little newborn lamb —especially as sacrificial animal in numerous acts of worship— is *amnós*. When worship is not the primary reference but is only secondary, the lamb, as an animal for slaughter, is called *arên*. The diminutive *arníon* originally meant the little lamb; later, as *amnós*, it came to signify the lamb.

All this semantic effort allows us to approach theological reflection with a stronger base, for it is a commonly accepted point in Biblical exegesis that in their own theological context, the people of Israel and the Christian community are often compared metaphorically to a flock of sheep *(próbata)*, and both Yahweh's Servant and Jesus —as we saw above— are occasionally compared to a lamb *(amnós* and *arníon)*.

The designation of Jesus as lamb *(amnós)* appears four times in the New Testament: Jn. 1:29 and 36, Acts 8:32, 1 Pet. 1:19. The key text is certainly the one of the Gospel of John, in which the Baptist designates Jesus, whom he has recently baptized, as the *lamb of God (amnós tou theou)*. Here, then, is the key to the characteristic understanding of Jesus as lamb: he is not simply compared to a lamb, as is the Servant of Yahweh in Isaiah's text, but is declared to be the lamb of God.

The Baptist's expression remains most surprising and worthy of reflection. If the word *lamb* is understood in its sacrificial meaning (or if the word *lamb* is replaced with the word *sacrifice)*, a whole new hermeneutic line is opened which permits a closer approximation to the New Testament understanding of the figure of Jesus in the economy of salvation.

In calling Jesus «the lamb of God» the evangelist seems to be having the Baptist say that all the sacrifices by humans will not eliminate the sin of the world, and that therefore, in the end of times, God delivers God's only Son, without sparing him, to save sinful humankind. God delivers him to the incarnation, and also to a vulnerable and mortal condition —the human condition. The Baptist's words (John 1:29), according to the exegetes, presuppose the baptism of Jesus (John 1:32-34) as his «yes» to the mission which will place him in the midst of a world crisscrossed by sin and violence, in order to live out and practice there an unconditional and unmeasurable love.

This means an anticipated «yes» to all the consequences that this delivery would imply. It is also a «yes» to the cross. The Father confirms the beloved Son in delivering him, and thereby inaugurates the eschatological time of salvation. Thus, by calling Jesus the «lamb of God», the text of John emphasizes the redemptive force of his death which takes away and obliterates the sin of the world.

Other passages in the New Testament highlight other aspects of Jesus as the lamb of God. Acts 8:32 points out his patience in suffering (similar to the Servant in Isaiah 53:7), while 1 Peter 1:19 —inspired by the ritual of the Passover lamb as it appears in the book of Exodus and by the entirety of the religious life of the People of Israel in the Old Testament— underlines the sinlessness and perfection of the sacrifice of Jesus in declaring him the «lamb without defect or blemish».

The text in Revelations brings a different perspective to the designation of Jesus as Lamb. The word *arnion* appears 27 times there, but not in the diminutive form. There Jesus is the Lamb, but an eternally beheaded lamb who is at the same time the judge of the world. Yet the author of this last book of the Bible strongly emphasizes the linkage of Jesus's triumphal condition with the fact that he is so glorious because he is the one who dies for us, and in dying saves us. In this one who triumphs and judges over all, the wounds of torture and death on the cross can still be seen. This is how the beheaded lamb, with his blood, acquired for God all of humankind with all its races and differences.

Thus the expression *amnós tou theou* («Lamb of God») designates, in the New Testament, the Gift that God offers in sacrifice, which is Christ himself, whom God designated to take upon himself the sin of the world and its deadly destructive violence. And the word *arnion* points to the identity of the eschatological Lord as the Christ, the victim of violence, who died on the cross for us.

A passage in John 1:29-34 puts in the mouth of John the Baptist an explicit reference to Jesus as the Lamb of God. To this the evangelist adds, in the mouth of the same John, the salvific mission of Jesus, the Lamb: to take away the sin of the world (v. 29). The evidence that this refers to the expiatory and vicarious death of Jesus is supported by other texts (1 John 3:5, 2:2, 4:10, 1:7, 5:6). The Lamb of God does not eliminate sin *from* the world —he does not build an idyllic and perfect world where conflict and confrontation have no place. But he does take away the sin *of* the world, that is, of all humankind. This is all that can be understood in the light of the Easter mystery.

Neither can the figure of the Easter Lamb be excluded from this hermeneutic line, in view of the major role it plays in early Christianity. According to John 19:36 it links the death of Jesus to the immolation in the temple of the Jewish Passover lamb —without any broken bones— at the same hour. But the meaning of the Crucified as the true Easter Lamb will be different from that of the Jewish sacrificial lambs.

John's followers associate the New Testament Easter Lamb with the idea of Jesus's expiatory death. In so doing they affirm that *this* lamb effaces the sins of the world. Because of this, no other sacrificial lamb, nor an expiatory goat of any kind, is needed. The mission of the Easter Lamb is not to suppress individual sins, but rather to bring a definitive end to the empire of sin. The one who takes away sin, who provides *forgiveness*—the only one who can do this— is God. And Jesus is the lamb that God provides now to take away the sin of the world —the lamb given by God, the lamb coming from God, the lamb *of* God.

With the presence of the Messiah —the Lamb of God— the promise of salvation is realized and God concedes to Israel and the world the fulness of forgiveness and reconciliation. Here Jesus is not the new ritual victim but the One through whom God intervenes, offering to humankind the perfect reconciliation with God.

Although the exegetes are slow in coming to an agreement regarding a direct link between the «lamb of God» and the «servant of Yahweh» of Isaiah 53, we believe we can state, with some of the most respected among them, that the expression «lamb of God», so fitting in the fourth gospel, invokes a reference to God's service as described in Isaiah 53, —a truly important text for the understanding of Jesus as the Messiah, for Jesus himself and for the the Christian community. Schnackenburg affirms that under the influence of the idea of the Passover, and perhaps also of the double meaning of «servant of God», the expression «lamb of God» came into use, and now embodies the content and meaning of both figures («servant» and «lamb»). The fourth evangelist, in describing the Baptist's witness of the messiahship of Jesus, perhaps wanted to convey immediately to his readers the singularity of this messiahship by offering the historical account and the Christian interpretation as together and inseparable.

But the truth is that there are fundamental differences between the two figures, the «lamb» and the «servant». Even if the evangelist hears, or can hear, in the Baptist message an echo of the Deutero Isaiah's lamb being taken to slaughter and not opening its mouth, there is a central difference. In Isaiah's prophecy the lamb atones for or «carries» the sin of Israel. Unlike the lamb of God in the fourth gospel, it does not take the sin away.

Israel's painful waiting comes to an end with the manifestation of Jesus who —whether interpreted as the Lamb who gives his life out of fidelity to God and human beings, or as the victorious Lamb of Revelations, or even as the liberating Easter Lamb— is fundamentally the One through whom definitive peace and reconciliation come to us. He is the One who vanquishes the violence of sin and makes the definitive light of the Kingdom of God shine upon humankind.

Thus Jesus Christ, the exalted Lord at the right hand of the Father God, the Second Person of the Holiest Trinity, is inseparably the servant who emptied himself of the glorious prerogatives of his divine condition, to follow a way of obedience that will take him to the sacrifice on the cross (cf. Phil. 2:5ff). He is the Lamb that by his sacrifice takes away the sin of the world (John 1:29, Acts 8:32, 1 Peter 1:19). This means, for all Christians, that to follow the way of Jesus Christ is inevitably to enter into his obedience, into his humble service, into his fidelity to *Abba*=Father until his death on the cross, and into his love for the brothers and sisters to the point of giving life for them. Only thus could they participate in his glory, in the way determined by God's infinite wisdom and sovereignty.

5

Jesus Christ: the Savior of the Present and the Future

The figure of Jesus Christ in the New Testament constantly links the present and the future. It is not a dualistic figure, couched in an opposition between the earthly and the heavenly. In the person of Jesus Christ, the earthly and the heavenly are definitively reconciled in a happy synthesis of God and humans, the Word and perfect obedient listening, revelation and faith, history and interpretation of faith, the earth and the heavens, flesh and spirit.

Therefore the same —and the only— salvation is already there in its fulness, affecting and redeeming the body of each individual, the body of society and the Church, as well as of men and women. Not only that, but it is also the eschatological promise. Just as the original creation, brought about by God in Christ, is always a current reality, so also is heaven already present on earth, which has been definitively invaded by them through the incarnation of the Word. So also will the earth be eschatologically transformed by that which already arrived through the incarnation, life, death and resurrection of Jesus Christ, and by his presence which establishes a new network of relationships and inaugurates a new cosmos.

At issue here is a world in which the Eucharistic banquet reunites all in a brotherly and sisterly interaction, in which everyone has a part without detriment to the others. The metaphor of the banquet, often used by Jesus himself, reveals in an excellent way what the salvation in Jesus Christ is, since in him is revealed not only what God wants and does on behalf of men and women, but also what God is. God is neither a theorem nor a logical mystery, but the mystery of salvation, the mystery of a fellowship that attracts and enables, in God's Son Jesus Christ, the access to profound communion with God.

This salvation takes place in a world burdened by conflict and death, and therefore its manifestations are precarious and often fragile. However, by looking at Jesus we can accept this heavy combat and unrelenting struggle with the same spirit as the Servant of God who emptied himself and was obedient until death, while taking upon himself the violence and sin of the world. Thus Christians will have the fortitude to stand on their feet, well grounded in the present and with their eyes full of hope, facing that horizon fully occupied by Jesus Christ as the conqueror of sin and of all evil.

6

The Relationship Between the Father and the Son in the Theologies of the New Testament

In view of what we have seen so far, the theme of the deity of Jesus Christ and of the relationship between the Father and the Son in the texts of the New Testament is serious and delicate, and thus calls for a reflection equally serious and profound. What is in play here is nothing less than the entire edifice of our faith and the conception of our salvation.

1. *If Jesus Christ were not God,* his words would be a representation of God, but would not be divine. The words of Jesus Christ would be like of those of the Buddha, Confucius and Mohammad. His acts, passions and Passion would have been felt *because of* God, but not *by* God. This makes a considerable difference in theological terms. For if God didn't touch life, death and suffering inwardly, our salvation would be seriously compromised and even questioned.

However, denial of the direct affirmation, «Jesus Christ is God», could make theological sense if it meant or implied, «Jesus is fully human», or, «Jesus is not God as the Father is God», or even, «God is also God in the mouth and heart of Jesus».

Reading the New Testament texts we clearly see that the evangelists were always careful to show that Jesus did not confuse himself with or place himself above the Father. On the contrary, he was a different person. Even when recognized and confessed as the Son of God, he is worshiped and adored as a divine person, but different from the Father. In other words, God is also God in the mouth of Jesus.

Jesus invokes God as *Abba* and does so in a characteristic way (4 times in Mark, 7 in Luke, 22 in Matthew). But in so doing, he subtly introduces to the disciples a relational difference that distinguishes «my Father» (Mark 14:36, Matthew 11:25) and «your Father» (Luke 6:36, 12:30 and 32, Mark 11:25, Matthew 28:9). His relationship with the Father is not the same as that which the disciples can have with the same Father. The disciples can call God their Father because Jesus opened the way for them.

The Our Father is the prayer of Jesus, but —more than that— it is the prayer that Jesus will teach his disciples: «Pray then in this way: Our Father…» (Matthew 6:9, Luke 11:2). This is an answer by the Master to a question from the disciples. But he does not thereby «transfer» to them the totality of the relationship that exists between the Son and the Father, which is unique.

In John 20:17, in the appearance to Mary Magdalene, we find the classic formulation of the theological point we just explained: «Do not hold unto me … But go to my brothers and say to them, "I am ascending to my Father and your Father, to my God and your God"».

In this exclusive «My Father» one finds the expression of a special relationship of Jesus with God which is not transferable and which continually reveals his filial life and consciousness. All of us are God's children (Matthew 5:9, 45). But he is so in a special and unique way. He is *the* Son. In him, and in him only, are we sons and daughters of God. We are by grace what He is by nature. We are the image and likeness of God. He is consubstantial —of the same divine substance— with the Father.

What the Gospels tell us, therefore, appears in the form of a *unity-otherness tension of Jesus with God.*

There are, for example, texts that emphasize the unity of Jesus with the Father. Jesus talks about the Father and with the Father as one who is equal in importance and dignity: John 10:29-30, 14:9ff, 17:1ff. Others highlight the otherness, the difference between Jesus and the Father. Jesus talks about and to the Father, but keeping a respectful and reverent distance, expressed in absolute and loving filial obedience: John 14:28, 5:19ff, and 30, 7:16, 6:57, 8:28.

From this dialectical tension between otherness and unity will emerge an understanding of the being, of the identity, of Jesus which will keep revealing itself as divine without ceasing to be human. The evangelists will keep delineating for us the map of their own experience, putting affirmations in the mouth of Jesus regarding his own being which will necessarily apply to the being of God.

There are, especially in the Gospel of John, some passages which are meaningful for the understanding of what we just said. In these passages Jesus is portrayed as talking about himself:

1. *I AM* (absolute, without a predicate):
John 8:24, 28 and 58, 4:26, 6:20, 13:19, 18:5-6.
The same is true of these other passages:
2. *I AM*, but with a predicate:
John 6:35, 48, 41, 51 («the bread of life»);
John 8:12 («the light of the world»);
John 10:7-9 («the door»);
John 15:1ff («the vine»);
John 11:25 («the resurrection and the life»);
John 10:11-14 («the shepherd»);
John 14:6 («the way»).

Each one of these predicates receives its meaning to the extent that it participates in the full meaning of the One who embodies it, or better said, the One who is. The «I am» of Jesus is like the «I am» of Yahweh in the Old Testament. For the evangelists, therefore, it is very clear that Jesus is not only the revealer of God, but is also the revelation. He is the real God. But the implicit ways to arrive at this experience of revelation and faith are not unveiled at just any moment. This relational tension of otherness-unity implies a divine identity that unveils itself only slowly. Jesus himself is the One who sets the moment. As Peter was told, in John 13:6-7, «You do not know now what I am doing, but later you will understand».

The reason for this is that the newness of this revelation demands a new human being, a new creature. As said in Mark 2:22ff, «No one sews a piece of unshrunk cloth on an old cloak ... and no one puts new wine into old wineskins».

The inquiry into the identity of Jesus Christ reformulates the inquiry into the identity of God and of the human being. And this is a reality so tremendous that it cannot be conveyed without a process of renewal and purification.

As John 3:3-7 says, narrating the conversation of Jesus with Nicodemus, «You must be born from above...» The newness is so radical and tremendous that it demands a new birth, a new creature. It demands being born again.

In truth, what the gospels are trying to tell us is that the human understanding of this «I AM» (that is, of the being of Jesus, of who Jesus is) will only come about when «the Son of Man be lifted up» (John 3:14-15, 8:28). And this «be lifted up» in the fourth Gospel refers to the hour of Jesus, the hour of his passage from the cross to Resurrection. This means that an understanding of the mutual identity between Jesus Christ and God, of Jesus Christ as the real God, presumes death and resurrection. It presumes entering into the dynamics of Easter, passing with Him from death to life, and afterwards retaking his whole history. That was what the early Christians and the Gospels did. And today we are called to do the same.

Therefore to affirm that the Resurrected is God makes sense only if the death of the man Jesus is concomitantly affirmed.

7
The Trinitarian Revelation in the Cross of Jesus Christ

The newness of the Christian Revelation of God calls for a new human being, a new creature. That is why in the Gospels we find the «messianic secret», namely, the enigmatic and mysterious answers by Jesus to questions concerning his identity and the identity of the God he revealed. He never gives a clear answer to these questions, but responds with another question or refers to a sign. In other words, he compels the interlocutor to continue the search on his or her own so that the revelation of God may happen to him or her.

This shows us that the revelation of Jesus as *Messiah-Christ-Son-God* was not something to be perceived easily even by those who lived closer to him. But it is also important to point out that such a revelation, besides being enigmatic, is scandalous. It demands that the person allow him or herself to be «re-made» by the Holy Spirit, in order to be able to perceive that in this man of flesh and bone lies the revelation of the real God. Apart from being an enigma and a scandal, this revelation engenders different reactions in the listeners. Jesus always answers in enigmatic ways, open to more than one interpretation. And the listeners cannot receive his answers quietly. Instead, his answers lead them to new questions which by themselves lead to new answers.

In this process of searching for answers to questions about the identity of Jesus Christ and the God whom he reveals, some of his contemporaries, listening to him, came to the *answer of faith*—HE IS THE SON OF GOD:

Mark 1:1 - the evangelist; Mark 1:11 - God the Father (the Baptism); Mark 9:7 - God the Father (the transfiguration); Mark 3:11 - the demons; Mark 5:7 - the demons; Mark 14:61 - the Council (question?); Mark 15:39 - the centurion; John 4:29 - the Samaritan; John 6:68-69 - Peter; John 9:35-38 - the man blind from birth; John 11:27 - Martha.

Others, on the contrary, came to the *anti-answers*:

Mark 2:7 - the blasphemer; Mark 3:21-30 - troubled, possessed by a demon; John 8:41, 9:16 - irreligious; John 5:16 - violator of the Sabbath; John 5:18 - blasphemous; John 7:12, 47-50 - agitator of the crowd; John 10:20 - madman; John 8:22 - suicidal; John 8:48 - the Samaritan; John 7:20, 8:48 and 52 - possessed by the demon.

The divergence of answers and anti-answers about Jesus proceeds in a «crescendo». This «crescendo» is both conflictive and revealing of the conflict taking shape around his person. The conflict keeps growing until the negative answers and the accusations finally prevail and lead him to the CROSS.

The conflict's motif, rather than political or any other thing, is above all religious. The accusers of Jesus are specialists in religion. They understand the implications of someone fully human performing actions which make him equal to God: healing on the Sabbath, forgiving sins, allowing his disciples to be above the Law, communing with the «godless», going outside the law by invoking His own authority, demanding renouncement of everything as the condition for following Him, having a unique and untransferable relationship with God.

The teachers of the law understand the reach of the fact that Jesus is trying to signify with his (human) behavior and words the involvement of God in human affairs (Mark 3:1-6, Matthew 5:43-48, John 5:15-18, John 10:31-38).

This *praxis* of Jesus, this behavior shored up by his *discourse,* is interpreted as diabolic (cf. Mark 3:22ff) by those who attribute to the Evil Spirit what Jesus does in the plenitude of the Holy Spirit. On the basis of such an interpretation Jesus must die. This conflict will lead to condemnation and death.

It is here that a great question arises: Jesus is arrested, accused, condemned, tortured and dies. Confronted with his death, faith is quiet and finds itself facing a perplexity.

How can one possibly elaborate a theological discourse from the perspective of the CROSS, if one must confront the Passion and Death of this one whom the cross recognizes as the Son of God and the real God? Theology must humbly remain quiet and wait to speak only later. For nobody can consciously state that *Jesus is God* without at the same time being aware that this Jesus in whom we believe is the *man* who was arrested, condemned, and tortured and who died, was buried, and was resurrected *by God*. Only then can one say: *that man was God*.

Only from the standpoint of his death and resurrection can we fully affirm: «Jesus Christ is of a divine nature!» That was the New Testament way.

Theology, facing the Cross, must therefore encounter perplexity in several questions for which there are apparently no answers:

1 What does God reveal of God's self in the passion and death of Jesus Christ? What kind of loving and merciful God is this who abandons God's Son to torture and death? who *delivers* the Son? (John 3:16, Rom. 8:32, 2 Cor. 5:21, Gal. 3:13 etc.)

2 How to combine the suffering and death of Jesus Christ on the Cross as the suffering *of God*, with the attributes of God in traditional Greek teachings such as «God is unchangeable», «God is impassive», «God cannot be touched by anything», «God is omnipotent» etc.? And more: how to make the episode of the cross, with all its dramatic and painful burden, coincide with the central affirmation of the New Testament: «God is love» (1 John 4:16)?

3 Can God suffer? Can God change? What does human suffering have to do with God?

4 Where is (was) God when Jesus Christ died? Where is (was) God when humankind, the righteous and the innocent suffer and die? Where does this God, who is love, hide?

The Church considers two possible answers:

1 *Jesus suffers on the cross, but he is not God* (this is the answer of the ebionites, adoptionists, arians and nestorians). The death of Jesus would have been suffered not by God but because of God. This affirmation brings into focus the problem of salvation. If God did not experience death, and did not touch death from the inside, how can we also be saved from it? Since only God has the power to save us, what becomes of our salvation if God does not enter with us into death's bottomless and wordless abyss?

2 *Jesus is God and does not suffer* (this is the answer of the docetists, apollinarians, modalinists, monophysites etc.). This answer indicates that what we see in the cross and in the death of Jesus has nothing to do with God, who remains outside all that happens there. His humanity there is only appearance. It is

not part of the identity of the Son of God, which could neither be touched by nor altered by suffering and death.

There is also a classic theologic answer: in the person of Jesus Christ two natures coexist. In the cross his human nature suffers and dies, while his divine nature is preserved.

Yet some precautions are necessary for a good understanding of this answer of the Church. Couldn't one fall into the risk of taking one nature as one person? In other words, couldn't one fall into the risk of making each nature (the divine and the human) so independent of each other as to be seen as two distinct persons? If that were the case, what would become of the other fundamental affirmations of the Christian faith, such as, for example, the one that calls Mary *Theotokos* (the mother of God)? The ecclesial affirmation of faith coming from the Council of Ephesus (431 CE) does not say that Mary is the mother of Jesus Christ only in his human nature, and yet he happens to be God. It rather says that Mary is the mother of God.

Furthermore, any equivocal interpretation of the two natures doctrine leaves unanswered the question of human suffering. Why does faith tell us that the Cross of Jesus is normative for explaining this issue? Is it also normative for the definitive explanation of the Trinitarian revelation of God?

The early Christian community sensed the truth of the cross as the Trinitarian history of God. It sensed that one can only conceive the extent of this mystery by looking at the Crucified. This is what opens the way for looking as well at the God whom He calls Father and at the Spirit who moved him during his life and is delivered by him at the moment of his death. Underlying the narratives of the Passion is a structure supported by the frequent appearance of the verb *to deliver* (*paradidomi*—*paradidonai* in Greek), which gives us a key to the reading of the story.

In the passion narrative, along with the trial of Jesus—to which he is delivered by Judas, by the Council and by Pilate— the Christian community perceives through faith, writes about, and witnesses three other *mysterious deliveries* which give meaning to the mystery as a whole.

a) *The delivery that the Son makes of himself* to the Father, for love (Gal. 2:20, 1:4, 1 Tim. 2:6, Titus 2:14, Eph. 5:2, 5:25, Lk. 23:46, John 19:30). In seeing and experiencing the delivery of the Son to the Father, one sees and experiences what occurs in the deeper mystery of the relationship between the Son and the Father. The Son enters into the deepest profundity of the world's sin and pain —that is, into that most distant place of the suffering of Godless humankind— to assume all of this in the Easter offering and reconciliation (Gal. 3:13f., Mk.15:34, Mt. 27:46).

b) *The delivery by the Father* (it is important here to pay attention to the passive tense of the verb, the «divine passive», which says that «Jesus, the Son, *is delivered*». In other words, a passivity, also present in God, is shown in the person of the Son) —(Mk. 9:31, 10:33 and 45, Mk. 14:41f, Mt. 26:45b-46). God, the Father of Jesus, delivers him (John 3:16, Rom. 8:32, 1 Jn. 4:10, Rom. 5:6-11). The suffering of the Father in the passion of the Son is rooted in a delivery of love. God is love. This fundamental affirmation of the New Testament is pointed out in a privileged way in the painful offering and delivery that God the Father makes of the Son for the love of God's created humankind.

c) *The delivery of the Spirit* —the supreme act of delivery (Jn. 19:30) by the Crucified. The Spirit whom the Father had given him and who will be once again plentifully given in the resurrection, is delivered and poured over history. The time of sin and of death's victory is a time of absence of the Spirit, a time through which the Crucified and dead Son passes to make possible the return of sinners to the Father by the Son «on the third day» (2 Cor.5:21, Rm.2:3).

The Holy Spirit is, in the account of the Passion, what keeps alive the Trinitarian colloquy during the time of silence and the hour of darkness, when creation would sink into the gloom of primeval chaos. It is the Holy Spirit who testifies that this event of the Cross is an act that plays out *not away from*, but *in* God.

The Cross is, therefore, the Trinitarian history of God. The Trinitarian figure reveals itself in the unity of the Son who delivers himself, the Father who delivers him, and the Spirit who is delivered by the Son and received by the Father. The Trinity assumes the world's exile, sadness and suffering, which accompany and result from sin, so that this exile, this sadness and this suffering may, through Easter, get into the homeland of Trinitarian fellowship. The Trinitarian confession is another name for our salvation.

Thus, the only Trinitarian interpretation of the passion and death of Jesus Christ is the one that affirms that in the act of delivering the Son to the Cross, the Father delivers himself as well. Both suffer on the Cross —the Son who dies abandoned by the Father, and the Father who suffers the death of the Son. At the depth of the separation, amidst the most absolute loneliness, lies the most profound communion. This communion is found in the Spirit, who in spite of, and because of, being «suffocated» and «overcome» by the power of darkness, keeps the Father-Son colloquy alive in the world as a gift to men and women of all times and places (Lk. 23:46, Mt. 27:50).

In the Cross, thanks to the obedience of the Son, lie the hope and salvation for humankind, because at the Cross total perdition and abandonment lie in God. The real God is on the Cross, abandoned, suffering, dead. God passed through death «away from the gate» and died the last of deaths. God *had* to suffer and die like that (Lk. 24:46) so that no one else would ever have to remain «away» from God. There is not a single human situation, no matter how negative or terrible, which has not been touched, assumed and redeemed by God.

In making such affirmations, theology is well aware that God's suffering is not like ours. It is not the result of imperfections and omissions like ours, nor of other similar faults. It is, rather, the result of love —a love made from activity and passivity. In a world of sin and violence, love *cannot* kill and destroy without at the same time deceiving itself. Love *can only* suffer, die and resist. Every time justice is violated, Love suffers. In the face of the suffering of the innocent, there is no other way for love, and no other way for God, except to plunge into the thicket of pain, on the side of the weak, of the most oppressed, and suffer with them. Only thus can one say that Love is history's ultimate goal, stronger than death. Only thus can one affirm that God is love.

God reaches down to the deepest profundity of suffering and death. The Son dies abandoned; the Father suffers the death of the Son; the Spirit, given by both, unveils a future of hope and salvation for the whole of creation. This compels theology to think in a new way about the mystery of God and its implications for faith.

Such a conception of God questions the Greek teachings regarding the understanding and interpretation that influenced the Christian theological tradition, especially those about immutability (no change) and impassivity (no suffering). Likewise it challenges the thinking according to which perfection lies in unity while multiplicity equals deterioration. The Cross where Jesus Christ, the Incarnate Son, was nailed, affects the whole Trinitarian community. To accept the Triune God is, therefore, to accept the idea that otherness, multiplicity and difference can be wholeness and perfection.

Therefore, from the standpoint of the death of Jesus, one cannot affirm that human suffering is always negative. It is also —and definitively— redeeming, ever since the moment it was felt in God's own innermost being. There is nothing in the world alien from God, nothing that is not assumed (and therefore not redeemed) by God, not even negativity and pain. In Jesus Christ, the Lamb of God, the obedient Son, one finds the passion of God that continues taking place in those crucified throughout history.

On the other hand, the resurrection is an experience of identity in contradiction, since the Resurrected is the Crucified. The one whom the witnesses saw defeated and dead is the same one who now comes in glory and triumphant.

Thus, Easter is an intervention *in* Jesus of Nazareth, *of* the God of Abraham, Isaac and Jacob, with power, *according to* the Spirit of Sanctity. That God who liberated the People of Israel from Egypt and guided them through the desert, establishing a covenant with them, is the same God whom Jesus Christ calls Father and who now, after the death of Jesus, fully reveals and manifests God's self, showing that God's Spirit is the only one capable of giving life in the place where death appeared to have won the battle. Easter is the history of all humankind, which has always struggled to shine a light on its contradictory destiny of being made for life but having to die. In entering human history, God reveals its ultimate meaning, thus turning Easter from being simply human history into the Trinitarian history of God.

Christ was resurrected by the Father. The initiative is, therefore, from God the Father, who once again is revealed by verbs in the passive voice: Acts 2:24, 3:15, 4:10, 5:30; 1 Thess. 1:10; 1 Cor. 6:14, 15:15; 2 Cor. 4.14; Gal. 1:1; Rom. 4:24, 10:9; 1 Pet. 1:21.

The Father takes a stand on the Crucified, proclaiming him Lord and Christ (Acts 2:36). The Father is recognizing, in the past life of the Nazarene, the history of the Son of God; in his present, the history of the Living One who overcomes death; in his future, the story of the Lord who will return in glory.

In the resurrection God reveals God's self as the Father of the incarnate, dead, and resurrected Son who will come again. God offers God's self as the Father of mercy who says YES to the Crucified Son, and in Him says the definitively liberating YES to all slaves of sin and death.

The resurrection is the YES that the God of Life says about the SON of God, and says in Him about us, as prisoners of death. That is why it is the center of faith (I Cor. 15:14).

The early *kerygma* says that Jesus Christ rose from the dead: Mk. 16:6; Mt. 27:64, 28:67; Lk. 24:6 and 34; 1 Thess. 4:14; 1 Cor. 15:3-5; Rom. 8:34; Jn.21:24.

And the fourth gospel puts in the mouth of Jesus the following words: «Destroy this temple, and in three days I will raise it up ... but he was speaking of the temple of his body.» (Jn. 2:19 and 21). Therefore, according to the New Testament, the active role of the Son in the Easter event does not contradict the Father's initiative. On the contrary, one component of the eternal obedience of the Son is the fact that he has, in himself, the life which is constantly given by the Father. Thus the proclamation «Jesus is risen, Jesus lives and is Lord» is always «to the glory of God the Father» (Phil. 2:11). On the other hand, the resurrection of Christ is not just a passive acceptance. It is also an assertive claim by God to God's history and human history.

Jesus, the *abandoned* (delivered by the infidelity of love —cf. Mk. 14:10), the *blasphemer* (delivered by the hatred of the representatives of the Law —cf. Mk. 15:1), the *subversive* (delivered by the authority of Caesar's representative —cf. Mk. 15:11), is the *Lord of life* (Rom. 5:12, 7:25).

Thus, in Him human beings find themselves freed from sin, from death and from the law. The Resurrected confirmed his past intention («No one takes [my life] from me, but I lay it down of my own accord», Jn.10:18; «Destroy this temple, and in three days I will raise it up», Jn. 2:19) and confused the wise people of this world (I Cor. 1:23ff). In the present he offers himself as the One who lives and gives life (Acts 1:3; Jn. 20:21). In the future he is the Lord of Glory, the first fruit of the new humankind (1 Cor. 15:20-28).

8

The Resurrection is Equally the History of the Spirit

It is by His own strength that Christ is risen again (1 Pet. 3:18, Rom. 1:4).

The Spirit is that one whom the Father gives to the Son that the Humble may be Exalted and the Crucified may live as the Resurrected. It is as well what the Lord Jesus gives, according to his promise (Jn. 14:16, 15:26, 16:7; Acts 2:32ff).

The Spirit, in the Easter Event, is a double link, namely, of God with Christ, raising him from the Dead; and of the Resurrected with humankind, making it alive with a new life that never ends.

The Spirit is also the guarantor of the contradictory double identity of the Crucified as the Living One. The One seen dead by all is alive, and death no longer has power over Him. The Spirit guarantees that following the death and resurrection of Jesus, God the Father will not leave humankind orphaned. Each man and each woman will be inhabited by God and able to believe in Jesus Christ as well as to love and follow him, thus entering into communion with the true and living God.

A God who is Spirit and Dwells in Us

Light

You do not call us
to bring light to the darkness
with frail wicks
cosseted from the winds
by the palm of the hand,
nor to be pure mirrors
reflecting other lights,
sought-after stars
reliant on other suns
which, like masters of the night,
illuminate
with momentary reflections
mere surfaces
according to their whim.

You offer to be
the light within us (Matthew 5:14)
ardent bodies,
glowing with a flame that cannot die
in the marrow of the bone (Jeremiah 20: 9),
burning bushes
in future-questing
wasteland solitudes (Exodus 3: 2),
ember in the inglenook
gathering companions
who share in fish and bread (John 21: 9),
prophetic lightning
which fractures the night
that is so truly the mistress of death.

You offer to be
the light of the people (Isaiah 42: 6),
pentecostal pyres,
as our days
are relentlessly burned off,
ignited by your Spirit,
to be aglow in you
who are light,
inseparably melted,
our fire with your fire. ❦

BENJAMÍN GONZÁLEZ BUELTA, SJ *(p. 101)*

Christian theology affirms that the Spirit who was poured down in Pentecost, who calls and leads the church, who re-creates and transfigures the whole creation, leading it to its fulness, dwells in us. God's Spirit, the Third Person of the Holy Trinity, dwells in us. To experience this is the vocation of all Christians and the condition that enables them to live out their call, ministry and mission in the world.

The experience of the Holy Spirit —creator Spirit from before the creation of the world, Spirit of Jesus Christ, architect of the new creation, who dwells in the human being— subverts the most fundamental anthropological categories. In other words, the indwelling of the Spirit recreates the human person from inside, from his or her deepest profundity.

a) The first characteristic of this indwelling is the fact that the Holy Spirit provokes in the person an *exodus, a going out of oneself.* He or she feels a desire and a need to draw himself or herself out of the self, out of his or her most immediate concerns, comfort areas and attachments —and in so doing to give himself or herself fully to all others (1 Cor. 9:22) and to confront the most adverse situations, dangers and tribulations (2 Cor. 1:4ff, and 5ff, 8:2, Phl. 4:14 etc.), including rejection, suffering and death (2 Cor. 12, Gal. 2:19ff and 6:17, 1 Cor. 2:1-5 and others). In this way the Holy Spirit integrates human beings into their own self-emptying action, from the self-emptying of the Trinity who comes towards humankind to carry out the plan of salvation. If there is a *kênosis* (self emptying) of the Son —who, without presumption regarding his divine condition, humbles himself by assuming the human condition until his passion and death (Phil. 2:6-11)

—there is also a *kênosis* of the Holy Spirit, who merges with our spirit, moans in us, and helps us in our weaknesses (Rom. 8:16 and 26).

In anthropology one thus finds replicated the exodus of the Word who, although of a divine condition, did not insist on the prerogative of being equal to God, but became human —humble, obedient and a servant— until death on the cross (Phil. 2:5-11). Also replicated is the exodus of the Spirit, who is continually sent by the Father and by the Son as the «other» Paraclete, who has a mission of «reminding» and «reminiscing» concerning the words said by Jesus of Nazareth, and of guiding the listeners to the whole truth (cf. Jn. 16:13, 14:26, 15:26). Therefore, similarly to the continuous exiting of God from God's self, human beings —in contemplating and experiencing the Son of God and the Spirit of God coming toward the world and humankind from the ineffability of the intra-Trinitarian fellowship— proceed to become pilgrims (and to have a self understanding of themselves as pilgrims) without a place to lay their heads (Lk 9:58), without a permanent city, without finding themselves in themselves but only outside themselves, in the other and in the others.

b) The Spirit alters the interior and exterior spaces of human beings. This experience implies that the human being must live in the space of the other and allow the other to live in his or her own space. This has several serious implications and consequences at all levels. On the one hand, this permanent alteration of space means that one is always going in unknown directions and opening oneself to invasion by the unknown. The other is a mystery never fully unveiled. To be ready to live in the space of the other is to expose oneself to being rejected, suffocated, saddened, vilified and even eliminated (cf. Gal. 5:17, Eph. 4:30, 1 Thess. 5:19, Heb. 10:29). It is to remain anonymous and obscure in an alien space, like a grain of wheat that must die in order to bear fruit (cf. Jn. 12:24). It is to assume the other's characteristics, culture and categories, and from that standpoint to announce the good news without imposing on it extraneous categories that would hinder access to communication from the Spirit (Acts 17:16ff).

On the other hand, one finds positive consequences in the concrete production of an alternative space for the human being. The Spirit who alters the anthropological categories is a Spirit who takes human beings away from themselves to place them in an «other» space. In the biblical way of thinking, space is a fundamental way to self understanding for human beings. The loss of one's bearings, place, land, space —the «atopic» condition— is always felt and experienced as misfortune and curse. The divine question to Adam, after the fall,

«Where are you?» (Gen. 3:9), doesn't refer simply to place understood as physical and geographical space, but to the whole existential situation of the human being. Cain's curse of being a wanderer in the world, without a land, without a space, without a place (Gen. 4:11-12), makes evident how primordial space was, as an anthropological category, for the biblical human beings.

The Holy Spirit, in altering and subverting human space, prevents human beings from continuing to understand themselves from their own point of view and from defending, with tooth and nail, their «own» space, by placing them *in Christ.* The destiny of those indwelt by the Holy Spirit is not one of losing «their» place and becoming wanderers in the world, without a place to go. On the contrary, it is one of discovering for themselves a new situation, a new place, another land, another homeland, another landscape —as *christic* spaces. Through indwelling, the Spirit takes human beings out of themselves in order to place them *in Christ,* thus making it possible for them to discover and to live out a new fellowship *in the body of Christ,* in community.

The real subversion that the indwelling accomplishes is truly christological, christic. This is so because the Spirit, by definition, is the one who «has no place». The Spirit's place is the Christ, the Anointed One, the Messiah (Mt. 3:16, Lk. 1:35); it is the human being as the Spirit's temple and residence (Eph. 2:22, 1 Cor. 3:16); it is the community, the Church, the Body of Christ (1 Cor. 12:13). In altering anthropological space, the Spirit, through the body and mouth of the one indwelt by the Spirit, opens a new space where anthropology can be subverted and reconstructed on the inside and the outside by Christology. A space, in short, where the human being can be another Christ.

c) The Spirit also alters the notion of *time.* For those indwelt by the Holy Spirit, time is no longer linear (*kronos*). It is rather a *kairós* (God's time), a time which has its unit of measure only in God. Thus understood it is a no longer a time that is subject to decadence (2 Cor. 5:17).

For this reason nothing can be measured any longer according to past temporal parameters. Paul severely admonishes the Galatians about this (Gal. 6:15, 4:8-11). Christians are not simply waiting for a new heaven and a new earth (1 Pet. 3:13), but are already living out a new order of things, a new creation. And although the painful «birthing» of this new order is still in process (cf. Rom. 8:21ff), the truth is that for those who live in Christ this new order is already a reality. For them the fulness of times is already here. It is the Spirit who brings it about and bears witness to this new situation, to all these things that are made new, by turning all into new creatures and new children. For even if on the outside human beings get old and are subject to the ravages of time, in their inner selves they grow and develop themselves rigorously until they reach the stature of Christ.

d) The Spirit also alters the category of *norms*. Human beings need and desire norms. They have no inclination for either anomy or anarchy. Yet Paul insistently asks the Galatians: «Did you receive the Spirit by doing the works of the law or by believing what you heard?» (Gal. 3:2). For those indwelt by the Spirit the law has meaning and strength only as a pedagogue of the Covenant. But those already living the Good News of Christ experience the fulfillment of the promise and the plenitude of love.

Therefore there is a norm for those indwelt by the Spirit and those who are in Christ: the freedom that comes from love. In that same letter to the Galatians, Paul says: «For freedom Christ has set us free. Stand firm, therefore, and do not submit again to a yoke of slavery» (Gal. 5:1). This freedom, against which no law has power, finds its security in the gift of the Spirit that inhabits human hearts. «Where the Spirit of the Lord is, there is freedom» (2 Cor. 3:17).

However, this love that generates freedom is not free from conditions (Gal. 5:13ff). But such conditions are no longer felt as a heavy fog that separates one from God. They are rather felt as «logical» —or better said, mysterious— consequences for those who have entered a new dynamic of life no longer ruled by the law, but rather by that love which is now attainable by all. Those who love have fulfilled the law (Rom. 13:10), and against the fruits of the Spirit of love there is no law (Gal. 5:23).

e) Having altered the space, the time and the anthropological norm, the Sprit alters the *human form* as well. The New Testament is full of texts where this alteration by the Holy Spirit of form in the human being appears under different names: «seal» (Eph. 1:13 and 4:30), «image» (2 Cor. 3:18), «garment» (Col. 3:10; Eph. 4:24).

It is a true transformation, a metamorphosis brought about in human beings that will at the same time give them a new shape, a conformation to Christ.

The «trans-formation» which the inhabitation by the Holy Spirit brings about in a person is, indeed, a «con-formation». In being transformed by the Spirit of life and holiness, Christians are more and more «con-formed» to Jesus Christ: they are able to understand themselves only from the standpoint of Jesus Christ; they are unable to speak to the world and to the tribunals in words other than those of Christ; they carry on their bodies the marks of Jesus Christ (Gal. 6:17);

and finally, they are «a letter of Christ... written not with ink but with the Spirit of the living God, not on tablets of stone but on tablets of human hearts» (2 Cor. 3:3).

Led by the Holy Spirit, the more spiritual anthropology is, the more christic it is. The more it bears the seal of the Spirit, the more it shapes those involved in its process in conformity with the person of Christ. The more it gives witness to the Spirit, who is its source and architect, the more it produces, in the midst of the world and society, a community that is the Body of Christ.

For, if it is true that Jesus sends the Spirit, it is also true that the Spirit was already in action before Jesus. If it is true that the experience of the Spirit acquires different contours before and after Christ, it is also true that the Spirit is not absent in the Old Testament.

It is in this sense that Jn. 7:39 must be understood: «Now he said this about the Spirit, which believers in him were to receive; for as yet there was no Spirit, because Jesus was not yet glorified». This text should not be taken in a chronological sense. The Holy Spirit does not begin to exist with the death and resurrection of Jesus Christ. Similarly, Christ himself, Son of God, the second person of Trinity, is *pre existent* to the historical manifestation of the Spirit. The gift of Christ saves all of humankind since its beginning, even though the life and death of Jesus of Nazareth occur in a determinate time and space.

Thus, the function of the Spirit is that of interpreting the Verb incarnate in Jesus of Nazareth, of teaching «theo-logical» language, and of being the love of God that is forever pouring into human hearts. And the gifts of the Spirit are —so to speak— precisely the Spirit, who creates more primary anthropological categories, and gives us a new way to understand history, the Church and the humankind we belong to.

The messianic mission of Jesus is the action and fruit of the Spirit. One can therefore say that the Spirit precedes Christ historically. The Spirit was at the creation (Gen. 1:2), gives life to the messianic people (Jn 3:1-5, Acts 2:17ff), and recreates the new creation (Ezek. 36:26ff, 2 Cor. 3:3, 5:17, Ezek. 37, Rom. 8:11-28, 1 Tim. 3:16). Yet the Holy Spirit is the Spirit of Jesus Christ. The New Testament applies to Jesus Christ the Old Testament texts that refer to the Holy Spirit:

Mt. 1:18-20, Lk. 1:37: Jesus is conceived by the work of the Holy Spirit; Mk. 1:10: the beginning of Jesus's messianic ministry is presided by the Spirit; Mk. 1:12, Mt. 12:28, Lk. 4:14 and 18: Jesus acts through the Holy Spirit; Heb. 9:14: on the Cross he delivers himself to the Father in the Holy Spirit; Rom. 1:4, 8:11, 1 Cor. 15:45: Jesus becomes a life-giving Spirit.

Thus the Spirit is a gift from Christ while, at the same time, preceding the creation of the world. In the Spirit the Christ is conceived. The Spirit is the creator in the Father, and re-creator» of the world in the Son.

The universality of the Spirit goes beyond that of the Historical Jesus and that of the Glorious Lord. Wherever Jesus is not known or recognized, the Spirit is present, providing God's redemption and salvation in His place. The Spirit is present even in cultures and traditions where God is called by other names. The real effects in history and in human life are proof of this. The gifts of the Spirit (1 Cor. 12 and 13) and the fruits of the Spirit (Gl. 5:22-24) are not dependent on an explicit belief in Christ or on membership in a particular church.

Nevertheless, we believe that the Holy Spirit is the Spirit of Christ. To be in the Spirit is to be in Christ, and only through the Spirit can we be in Christ (cf. Rom. 8:8-9; Phil. 1:19; Gal. 4:6). The passages of John 14:26 and 16:13ff specifically call our attention to this point. These texts do not deal with a reminiscence, but with a very lively present. Ultimately the Spirit has nothing to say which is not related to the resurrected Jesus who is alive in the community.

The Spirit is a person, a personal presence of God in the world, related to the Father and to the Son. The Spirit as the creator and source of life and as the Spirit of Jesus Christ is a unique general newness. The Spirit comes from the Father and arrives at the fulness of times in Jesus Christ. A «posterior» activity of the Holy Spirit was the universalization of the reality of Jesus Christ, the integration of all reality in him, the reconciliation of that reality with the image of God, and the making of humankind into the image of the New Adam as manifested in Jesus Christ—thus making possible the realization of the New Testament.

2

The Holy Spirit at the Creation

The Holy Spirit accompanies the entire work of creation from beginning to end. Like an impetuous wind, the Spirit blows over the primordial waters, causing life to emerge from them (Gen. 1:2). With the Church, the spouse of the Lamb, the Spirit asks the Lord to come and restore the whole universe (Rev. 22:17).

Together with the Father and the Son, the Holy Spirit is creator of all things. The Father creates everything in the image of the Son, with the strength and power of the Spirit. Because of this, the whole universe has the mark of the Holy

Spirit. In the Creed we confess: «I believe in the Holy Spirit, the Lord and life giver».

The Holy Spirit is the breath (in Hebrew *ruach*, which also means breathing, wind…) of God, the vital force, the divine energy that gives life to creatures. In Psalm 104:29-30 we recognize these words: «When you hide your face, they are dismayed; when you take away their breath, they die and return to their dust. When you send forth your spirit, they are created; and you renew the face of the ground.» Jesus confirms this revelation, saying: «It is the spirit that gives life…» (Jn. 6:63).

Thus we believe that the Holy Spirit of God preserves the world in freedom and love against all destructive chaotic powers. Furthermore, we believe that the Spirit is the real power of a new creation with a messianic hope for a new people with hearts fully turned to God (Ezek. 37:1-14). Since the time of Irenaeus, a Church Father of the second century, it has been part of the tradition of our faith to recognize that the Father creates with two hands —with the Word that was made flesh in Jesus of Nazareth, and with the Spirit or breath that brings life to the face of the earth.

The presence and action of the Holy Spirit in the work of creation have ethical implications for Christians. It is important for us to recognize the value of the world, because it was made good by its Creator (Gen. 1:10). The world participates in the goodness of God, and exists in God. The world is not a product of blind fate or chance, but of God's loving freedom. Therefore we should live with trust in God the Creator. God does not want to destroy the World, but to rebuild it in the strength of God's love. The contemplation of nature helps to nourish in us a remembrance of God and of our need to live in a loving relationship with God.

3

The Action of the Holy Spirit in the Church

In the community life of divine persons, the Spirit is, par excellence, love. In the creation of the world, in the history of humankind, in the religions and cultures of the people, in the hearts of human beings, in the fellowship and service of the Church, the Holy Spirit pours down the love that unceasingly encompasses the Trinitarian fellowship.

The relationship of the Spirit with the Church can be summarized by saying that the Holy Spirit is the soul of the Church. The Spirit is present in all that the Church is and does. The Spirit makes of the Church a most excellent arena for action, because it is here that the Spirit knows who can be counted on. The Holy Spirit is present and active in the so called three offices (or functions or ministries) of the Church, namely, the priestly, the prophetic and the royal, making of the whole Church and of each Christian a new Christ: a priest, a prophet and a king.

The Holy Spirit attends to the priesthood of the Church to ensure that the worship she offers to the Father is sincere and true —a worship that celebrates the life, death and resurrection of Jesus Christ; a worship that engages the life of all the people in their joys and sufferings; a living worship filled with a passion that touches the heart profoundly. In the celebration of each sacrament the Holy Spirit is invoked to ensure that all of Christian life is permeated by the climate of love and unity given to us by the Spirit.

The Spirit inspires the mission of the Church as she announces the Word. In the catechism, in the homilies, in the writings, in the formation of the clergy and lay leadership, in the documents of the Church, the Spirit illuminates and inspires Christians to remember the Word of Jesus and thereby produce the same effects as those produced by His preaching. It is also by the Spirit's power and strength that the Church denounces with emphatic words the sin of the world, offenses to human dignity, social injustice and religious indifference.

The Spirit enlightens the mission of the Church and all her efforts to be a community of brothers and sisters at the service of universal brotherhood and sisterhood. The Spirit distributes inside the Church many different gifts that allow the faithful to engage in ministries and service, perceive the needs and challenges of pastoral and evangelistic action, and be concerned with the properties as well as the administration of the communities, with social justice and the sharing of goods with all those in need.

Every Christian man and every Christian woman receives from the Spirit at his or her baptism one or more gifts to be placed at the service of the Church and the Kingdom of God in the exercise of his or her ministry.

The Church is the part of humankind that explicitly assumes the good news brought by Jesus Christ and his gospel. The Spirit, the Lord of the Church, assists her continually throughout the ages, in the midst of cultures and different historical eras, placing her always at the service of the plan of God's Kingdom, while eradicating her sin with divine holiness, that is, with the Holy Spirit. In presiding over the Church, the Spirit takes her beyond her contingency and vulnerability to become more and more the image of the Trinitarian community of the Father, the Son and the Holy Spirit.

The first Christians had the experience of being indwelt and moved by this divine Spirit of love, who taught them and helped them to live out the love taught and practiced by Jesus. As we are told in the Acts of the Apostles, in the first portrayal of the community, the first Christians «devoted themselves to the apostles' teaching and fellowship, to the breaking of bread and the prayers... All who believed were together and had all things in common; they would sell their possessions and goods and distribute the proceeds to all, as any had need» (Acts 2:42,44-45). A little further on, in another portrayal, it is reported that «the whole group of those who believed were of one heart and soul» (Acts 4:32). The first Christian communities received from Jesus and his disciples the call to live on earth in the same way the Holiest Trinity lived in heaven. Quite apart from doctrinal formulas and an intellectual eagerness to understand in their heads this mystery of faith, the first Christians, moved by the Holy Spirit, simply embraced the way of Jesus —living out their love for one another as one single heart and one single soul, and working incessantly to do the will of the Father, as Jesus did. In that way they experienced the indescribable grace of participating intimately in the life of the Holiest Trinity.

4

The Divine Person of the Holy Spirit

All of us manage to have some analogical and approximate idea of the divine persons of the Father and the Son. All of us are sons and daughters, and have a father. Many of us are fathers and have children. The words father and child belong to our familial language. It is more difficult for us to come up with an idea of the Divine Person of the Holy Spirit. The images that the Bible uses —fire, wind, water, oil, cloud, dove— indicate movement, fluidity, freedom. These are images that bring to mind the impossibility of apprehending and confining the Holy Spirit. We are left without a definitive, accessible and perfect idea of this Divine Person.

In Church tradition the Holy Spirit is the tie of love between the Father and the Son. If the Father is the eternal Lover of the Son, and if the Son is the eternal loved one of the Father, the Holy Spirit is the love between them both —the total and perfect Love that the Father gives the Son, and the total and full love that the grateful and obedient Son receives from the Father. For this reason we say that the Holy Spirit is both the Spirit of the Father and the Spirit of the Son. The Spirit's identity is precisely that of being and living on behalf of the other two, that they may love one another, while identifying with one another and distinguishing themselves from one other, as Father and Son.

The Holy Spirit is, therefore, the tie that enhances and clarifies the love between the Father and the Son. This way of being is what truly identifies and distinguishes the Holy Spirit as a person. The Holy Spirit is what the Spirit does: loves. The Spirit does what the Spirit is: love! And all that the Spirit is and does in the intimacy of the Trinitarian divine fellowship, is what the Spirit is and does in extra-Trinitarian relationships and accomplishments.

In the Spirit the teachings of Jesus are realized in a full and eternal way: «those who want to save their life will lose it, and those who lose their life for my sake… will save it» (Mk.. 8:35, Lk. 9:24). This means that only those who experience «love-service» or «love-sacrifice» will have an idea —even a dim one— of who the Holy Spirit is.

With the Holy Spirit we learn to be human and Christian. The Spirit teaches us that to live is simply to love. The nucleus of the human personality and, fundamentally, of the Christian, is love, humility in service, a propensity to do good, and self denial for the sake of others. In a world that exalts power and reason and encourages the pursuit of success and consumerism, of having and getting, of power and ruling, the Spirit teaches us that to be human and to be Christian is to place ourselves at the back of the line, at the root of history, in the breaches of conflicts, in the silence of the absurd, that everything may return to the way of love and service.

A Disarmed God

1

God Cast Off

In your Son, Jesus,
you cast yourself off,
quit eternity
for the harshness of the elements,
and in a spoiled inheritance,
human with us, and divine,
your love nested a flight
on wings of solidarity,
veering towards the heights,
ceaselessly lifting the horizon.

In your Son, Jesus,
you cast yourself off,
you took flesh to utter your closeness,
in the unheard-of pretension
of being all tongues and colours
in a flesh that is mortal and abridged,
of being a never-ending parable
of infinite inflexions for the ages,
turning up alive and pristine for all
at the lintel of the senses.
In your Son, Jesus,
you cast yourself off,
you risked your all with the lowly,
watched-over, the excluded and failed,
to tender us Life
in vulnerable meetings,
and that defenceless cheek,
sometimes kissed in friendship,
ultimately crushed beyond remedy
all the way to ridicule and death.

In your Son, Jesus,

you cast yourself off,

not imposing yourself , with theophanies,

with fires and sidereal frights,

nor with cunning seduction,

nor armed force,

for only in free finding

are dawns engendered

to rise up from the night,

and break more divinely.

BENJAMÍN GONZÁLEZ BUELTA, SJ *(p. 80)*

128 One of the most urgent questions for the human being today is how to talk about God in a world where peace seems to have become a remote —if not forever lost—reality.

Some contemporary Christian theologians can help us perceive the obstacles and clues that may lead us to articulate a conception of God compatible with the atmosphere of fear now surrounding humankind, especially after September 11, 2001. We will try to demonstrate that one can still believe that peace is possible. Furthermore, one can still talk about a God who anticipates and is encompassed by peace and justice.

2

Talking About God After Auschwitz

The holocaust (*shoá*), the biggest genocide ever in recorded human history, revealed, among other things, what human beings are capable of when possessed by the *hybris* of power and violence. To think about *shoá* is to look back at the most obscure and terrible dimension of human existence and realize that the human being is capable of producing a tragedy so enormous that we lack appropriate words to express its horror. The world was not the same after *shoá*. And John XXIII was certainly aware of this when he wrote his *Pacem in Terris* encyclical, less than twenty years later. In this genocide the Christian conscience felt itself severely questioned. And Christian theology, after remaining silent for some time, slowly began to ask itself:

1 How can we talk about God after Auschwitz? Raising this question is tantamount to searching for the real meaning of human existence. How can we proclaim an omnipotent and good God in view of such an unprecedented catastrophe? Can God be still called the Lord of history?

2 How was it possible for this tragedy to take place in Europe, in countries with a long Christian tradition? And to what extent did this tradition enhance or at least fail to prevent the eruption of anti-Semitism, and of Nazism and other regimes allied to it? What role did Christians and their churches play in those events?

According to some Jewish thinkers, among them Hans Jonas, it is impossible to talk about God after the holocaust while repeating God's traditional attributes of omnipotence, absolute goodness and understanding. But what then would be the alternative?

a) Instead of the biblical concept of divine majesty, Jonas puts forward a God who has suffered since the Creation. He bases this on the Jewish cabalist Isaac Lurian, who understood the act of Creation as painful contractions through which God gave birth to a Cosmos that was not God.

b) Instead of the biblical concept of a God who remains unchanging in perfection for all eternity, Jonas puts forward a God who, rather than coming into being as an indifferent eternity, grows over time with Creation.

c) Instead of a remote, exalted, and inaccessible God, Jonas puts forward a caring God, committed to those for whom God cares, one who takes risks to protect life.

d) Instead of omnipotence, Jonas puts forward the impotence of God. In Auschwitz and in all genocides on earth God remained silent and did not intervene, not because God did not want to, but because God could not. Jonas maintains the goodness and understanding of God, but relativizes God's omnipotence.

This is the challenge that deeply vexes some European Christian theologians. We will analyze two who confronted the challenge and dealt comprehensively with its questions. They are the German theologians J. Moltmann and E. Jüngel, who, looking at the wreckage of the Western world destroyed by Nazism, were moved by the urgent need to think of God in a different way.

2.1. JÜRGEN MOLTMANN AND THE CRUCIFIED GOD

Many Christians were disturbed by the controversy surrounding the existence of God and faith in God in the decades immediately following the Second World

War. These were years dominated by the Cold War, the Vietnam War and other major conflicts. Many believers in the God of the Judeo-Christian revelation found themselves disoriented in the face of such questions as «Did God die?» or «Can't God die?» or «Where is God, when humankind is destroying itself?». In the struggle for a new Church in a new society, some of them kept their distance from the problem of God. But soon a christological crisis began, regarding the definitive basis of support for Christianity. It highlights the problem of the real God and the identity of Jesus Christ: who is the God who motivates Christian existence —the crucified or the idols of religion, class or race? It seemed clear that without a new conception within the Christian faith there would be no credibility —after the controversies of recent years— for a discourse about the Christian God. Then, in a surprisingly new way, from the bosom of several Christian confessions, a number of converging tendencies of theological thinking emerged that made it possible to glimpse a new Christian doctrine about God.

The thinking that developed this doctrine is preceded by suffering. The problem of God emerges from the depths of the human being, from the pain of injustice and helpless suffering in the world. There are many movements and struggles for which history seeks an explanation: the struggle for power, class struggle, the struggle against racism, etc. But when one looks for a precise understanding of universal human history, the feeling is that it must be found among all the movements and conflicts that motivate it, that is, in the «history of the world's passion». In power humans differentiate among themselves, but in poverty solidarity reigns. In the positive they separate themselves, but in the negative they are all equal. The experience and perception of the pain of, and in, the world takes Christian theology beyond theism or atheism. In the face of the suffering of this world, it is sometimes very difficult to believe in the existence of an all powerful and merciful God who «magnificently rules everything». A faith that justifies suffering and injustice in the world without protest is inhuman and seems satanic. However, protest against injustice loses all its energy if it falls into a trivial atheism that reduces everything to this world and to limited intra-historic concrete situations.

The angry clamor for the *raison d'être* of faith is sustained by a longing for the «wholly Other». As Max Horkheimer says, it is «a deep longing in the human heart that the murderer should not triumph over the innocent victim». It is an irrepressible longing for justice. Without a passion for justice in the world and for the One who is indisputably its guarantor, there will be no conscious and proliferating suffering, caused by injustice, to motivate action to restore justice.

While suffering leads to the questioning of the idea of a just God, the longing for justice and its guarantor puts suffering under judgement, turning it into conscious suffering. Beyond theism and atheism, suffering and the protest against it lead us to the problem of theodicy: *Se Deus iustus, unde malum*? If we cry out for God in questioning why there is suffering, the reason for the question of God's existence —*an Deus sit?*— is experienced as suffering itself. Traditional theism answers this double question with the justification of this world as «God's world». This world, exactly as it is in reality, is a mirror of the deity. Such an answer is no longer either possible or satisfying. The mirror is broken by violence. For this reason such an answer implies idolatry.

Traditional atheism omits the existence of suffering as the basis for questioning God. «God's only excuse is that he does not exist», as Stendhal and Nietzsche said. Ironically, the non-existence of God becomes an excuse for a frustrated creation. But in practice it means that if human beings give up the habit of asking questions about ultimate meaning and justice, they will end up giving in to contentment and accommodation to the deficiencies of their circumstances.

Critical theology and critical atheism accept suffering as the starting point for the question of justice. Critical Christians and critical atheists meet each other in the struggle against injustice, irrespective of religious labels, in the context of practical solidarity. But at the level of the history of the world's passion, what does the history of Christ's passion mean? Before one can consider —and answer— this question one must clarify what the history of Christ's passion means for none other than God, and therefore for the Christian faith in God. A God who reigns from a heavenly throne, with an unconcerned happiness, is unacceptable. Wouldn't a God incapable of suffering also be a God incapable of loving, and therefore poorer than any human being? And what else can a God who suffers mean for suffering humans, other than a religious recognition of their pain?

Christian theology can expose the history of the world's passion only by going beyond theistic illusion and atheistic resignation. In the context of the history of Christ's passion, it recognizes the being of God in the death of Christ on the cross. Only by reflecting on what happens between the Crucified and «his» God can we realize what this God means for the afflicted and neglected of the earth.

Thus, the Cross is either the end of theology or the beginning of a specifically Christian theology. Christian language regarding God becomes, in the Cross of Christ, a Trinitarian language about the «history of God». It must distance itself from any monism, pantheism or polytheism. The centrality of the Crucified is the specifically Christian in universal history, just as the doctrine of the Trinity is the specifically Christian in the doctrine about God. They are both intimately related.

We take the exegetic content for this affirmation from Pauline theology. The Greek word for it *(paradidomi)* has, in the passion narrative of the Gospels, a clearly negative resonance. *Paradidomi* means to betray, to deliver, to abandon, to sacrifice, to kill. Paul uses this meaning in Romans 1:18ff, writing about God's abandonment of the atheists. Guilt and punishment coincide. Those who abandon God are abandoned by God and «delivered» to the ways they themselves chose: the Jews to their legalism and the heathen to their idolatry, and others, here and there, to death. Paul introduces a change in the meaning of *parédoken* («delivered») when writing about the abandonment of Jesus, no longer in the historical context of his life, but in the eschatological context of faith. The One who «did not withhold his own Son, but gave him up for all of us, will he not with him also give us everything else?» (Rom. 8:32). In the historical abandonment of the Crucified Paul sees the delivery of the Son by the Father on behalf of those distanced from God.

But in this context Paul also highlights the delivery of the Son to the Father. Jesus suffers death in abandonment by God. But the Father suffers the death of the Son in the pain of his love. If the Son is delivered by the Father, the Father suffers His own abandonment of the Son. The Japanese theologian Kazoh Kitamori called this mystery the «suffering of God». Since the suffering of the Son is distinct from the suffering of the Father, Moltmann understands this as a Trinitarian event, leaving aside for the moment the general concept of God. In Gal. 2:20 *parédoken* appears with Christ as the subject («…the Son of God , who loved me and gave himself for me»). According to the apostle, it is not only the Father who delivers the Son. The Son delivers himself to himself —a reference to the communion of wills between Jesus and the Father at the moment of his total separation in abandonment by God in the Cross. Paul had already interpreted as love the abandonment of Christ by God. This appears in the theology of John (3:16). And the first letter of John sees, centered in this event of love on the cross, the existence of God: «God is love» (4:16). In later terminology, one can speak —in relation to the cross— of a *homousía* or a co-substantiality of the Father with the Son, and vice-versa. On the cross, Jesus and his God and Father find themselves immensely distanced from each other by abandonment, and at the same time brought into the closest possible mutual unity by the delivery. That is because from the cross—between the Father who abandons and the abandoned Son—comes the real delivery, namely, the Spirit. The Father is the One who abandons and delivers. The Son is the abandoned one, delivered by the Father and also delivered by himself. From this historical-eschatological reality comes the Spirit of love and delivery, who comforts the destitute human beings. Thus we interpret the death of Christ not as an event between God and the human being, but above all as an intra-Trinitarian event between Jesus and his Father, from which the Spirit comes.

This Trinitarian language—still according to Moltmann—preserves the faith from both monotheism and atheism, keeping it bound to the Crucified and showing the cross as inserted into the being of God, and the being of God as inserted into the cross. The material principle of Trinitarian doctrine is the cross. The formal principle of the theology of the Cross is the Trinitarian doctrine. The unity of the history of Father, Son and Holy Spirit can therefore be called «God». With the word «God», Moltmann's theology seeks to express this event between Jesus, the Father and the Spirit as a distinctive history. It is the history of God, from which comes the revelation of who and what God is. Whoever wants to speak of God in a Christian way will have to «narrate» and preach the history of Christ as a history of God—as the history of the relationship of Father, Son and Spirit, which establishes who God is. This is true for human beings and is central to their existence. This means that the being of God is historical and exists in this concrete history. The «history of God» is, thus, the history of the history of the human being. Thus redemption, even from the harm caused by violence, and God's infinite mercy continue for everything in human history.

3

Eberhard Jüngel and the God who is the Mystery of the World

Jüngel's method is primarily established in his hermeneutic starting point. He is convinced that for an existential interpretation of Scripture it is important to think about faith in a way that will enable it to provide a reason for «the crucified God worthy of being thought about». This means, for Jüngel, giving up the metaphysics of substance, and especially the postulates about God taken from Greek metaphysics. For him theology should be supported only by faith, since only faith is beholden to the revelation of God in the Word of God. Likewise this calls for a new way of thinking about God, namely, from the perspective of the *verbum crucis* as the definitive word about Christ, and, in him, about God. This new paradigm moves from an ontology oriented to a metaphysics of substance to an ontology of actual event, subject and relationship. It has many advantages, including the fact that it «makes possible a better knowledge of the historicity of the assumption of the truth of the biblical texts», and it also «makes possible a sharper knowledge of the historicity of the God who comes into the world». Thus, Jüngel's theology about God finds its starting point in a theology of the cross. Christian theology is fundamentally, in this view, a theology of the Crucified, because God is identified with Him.

With this theological principle Jüngel wants to express two things: the first is the identification of God with the man Jesus who was executed on the shameful scaffold of the cross; the second is the consequent manifestation of the humanity of God. In God's humanity—brought about through identification with Jesus on the cross— the essence of the Christian God is revealed as a Trinity of persons. «Faith in the man Jesus crucified for us (meaning for a humankind which both deserves and brings about his death) as the Son of God, presupposes the identification of God with Jesus and the Trinitarian self-differentiation of God». This means that faith in Jesus as the Christ necessarily implicates God in the death of this man, otherwise it would not confess him as the true God in hypostatic unity with his humanity. At the same time, if God can experience death without succumbing to it, this is due to the auto-differentiation of God within the Trinitarian persons. The cross reveals in all its extremes the humanity of God, and that makes it possible for the destiny of humankind to be narrated like any historical fact.

In the word of the cross one also find the occurrence of our redemption: «The death of Jesus makes it clear that the law brought condemnation and that its curse was fulfilled... The death of Jesus shows that God justifies the sinner in that moment (cf. Rom. 4:5)». Thus Jüngel, following Luther —who learned it from St. Augustine— talks about the cross as a sacrament, and not simply as an example. The soteriological and ontological strength of the cross cannot be weakened by being considered a good example for the moral life of the Christian, even if seen as not excluding that.

In light of this, one can understand why in Jüngel everything begins with the concept of God as love. The treatment of God in the Christian faith must enhance a better understanding of the New Testament expression «God is love». Although apparently simple, this is the main task of theology, according to Jüngel. One can say that his whole theology from a material point of view focuses on God as love, while from a formal point of view it focuses on the identification of God with the Crucified. There is a circularity in the trilogy of affirmations that Jüngel holds as basic to his concept of God, affirmations that cannot be understood separately. They are 1) God identified God's self with the Crucified, 2) God is love, and 3) God is Trinity.

But if the being of God as love was fully revealed in the Son who died on the cross, how could love be defined? From the viewpoint of the Revelation of God in the Crucified, theology must define love from a material point of view as «the event of the unity of death and life on behalf of life», while from a formal point of view it must be defined as «the event of an ever greater self-denial in the heart of such a great self-reference». That is how God self-defines God's self in the Son. But why insist on the definition «God is love» as opposed to other definitions that appear in the New Testament? Jüngel holds that theology always gave priority to this definition because «in this way it could refer not only to a New Testament expression, but also to the event without which the New Testament would never have emerged, the death of Jesus and his resurrection from the dead by the action of God». In saying «God is love» the human being assumes the historicity of a love. Such historicity was made possible by the humanity of God in Jesus of Nazareth.

Explaining the definition of God as love implies seeing the way in which God and love identify with each other. For Jüngel this presupposes, on the one hand, fulfilling the essence of love, so that, although a characteristic of God, love is not viewed as contradicting what human beings experience as love; and on the other hand, doing justice to the being of God, so that God as love is distinguished from human love, ensuring that the word «God» is not superfluous in this connection. Although theologically one must distinguish God from love, the difference should not be ontological, otherwise one could define God without love. In defining the Christian God, the word love cannot be replaced by any other under the pretext that the subject of the sentence is all that gives meaning to the predicate. It is important to point out here that the New Testament does not say that God «has» or «gives» love, but that God «is» love. Jüngel finds only one possible way to understand the verb «to be» in the relationship God-love: to explain God via christology as a Trinity of persons.

The above analysis —showing that the human experience of love shouldn't contradict what we preach about God as love— reveals that love exposes lovers to a nothing, and moves between being and not being. One sees also that, in the experience of love, lovers receive a new being given by the loved one, and one feels that the strength of love is limited to the occurrence of love. This is the source of its strength, weakness and impotence. Love cannot impose itself except with and as love.

From this understanding, one can better interpret theologically the central affirmation of the Christian concept of God: God is love. The possibility of understanding the essence of God as love, and the Trinitarian being of God, depends on God's identity as the crucified Messiah. Therefore, according to Jüngel, only in history can God be known by the human being. And we know that Jesus is the history of God among us. The history of Jesus is the history in which God defines God's self as love. At the end of the history of Jesus, in his death, the essence of God is revealed in its fulness. It no longer makes sense to separate essence and existence in God, as the philosophy of modernity has done. The existence (history) of God defines God's essence (love) and both are inseparable in God's being. In the cross of Jesus the essence of love appears in its fulness: «unity of death and life on behalf of life» and «ever greater self-denial and giving in the midst of a great intra-Trinitarian self-reference».

The New Testament texts, especially the writings of John, tell us that love revealed itself in the sending of the Son as a gift from the Father. However, love still does not reveal itself in its fulness in the Father-Son relationship. God is the event of love opening itself up to a third one, the Spirit, who differs from Father and Son. Love occurs when God (Father), as the lover separated from the loved one (Son), not only loves God's self but also includes what is wholly different from God (the world and human being) through the work of the Spirit. Thus God is, in essence, love —an ever greater self-denial in the midst of the fellowship of the persons of the Trinity. But with this definition of God as love something is added to human love, since in the human being love takes place among persons who consider themselves worthy of being loved. In God this arrangement changes since there is no self love in the Spirit without love for the other —the human being who is sin, misery, injustice and death. Love is different in God because it is linked to the Crucified, which means that it is freely given to another who is not worthy of love. On the cross it delivers itself to the human being, who is a sinner and therefore not lovable. God loves not because the object is worthy of love. On the contrary, in loving the human being God makes him or her attractive and worthy of being loved.

Thus, in the dead and risen Jesus faith discovers God coming to meet the human being in a definitive way. Therefore Jüngel says that Jesus is, par excellence, the footprint of the Trinity, because without him the discourse about the Trinitarian God would be untenable speculation. According to Jüngel, what the Christian faith believes and the motive for its belief are found in the Easter mystery of Jesus. In identifying God's self with the one who suffered abandonment and violent death, God radically differentiated God's self and granted us salvation. There is no tension between self-affirmation and surrender in God. In love, affirming oneself and another is not conflictive because in love there is always greater self-denial, greater self-outpouring and greater self-offering.

The question remains: can God be impassive and immutable if God is love? A theology of the cross that is foundational for the doctrine of the Christian God must provide answers to the two great theological questions which are directly related to the concept of God: mutability (or immutability), and impassivity (or capacity for suffering). In light of the biblical texts about God's revelation, and especially in light of the Crucified, a different reading is needed of the theological principle of the immutability and impassivity of God. Jüngel will say that the being of God includes action, happening and movement in the inexhaustible wealth of God's intra-divine relations, without God ceasing to be God. The Trinitarian differentiation means that God meets in the Incarnation that which is not God, without the human and the divine thereby ceasing to be concordant in God. In the action of coming into the world, God does not cease to be God, because «God comes from God» and is Father, «God goes to God» and is Son, and God does this «as God» and therefore as Spirit. The revelation shows us the being of God in action, which is especially visible in God's decision to choose the human being (in the Son), from the beginning of eternity, as a partner in God's Covenant. God does not want to be God without us: «If God is thought of as the One who chooses, the being of God is therefore thought of as a being in action». This means that God's being is a historical being. A non-Trinitarian God would be a static God and would remain inaccessible to the human being, unable to reveal God's self historically. The being of God as «happening» allows one to think of God as the One who reveals God's self. It is love among the divine persons that makes possible the historicity of God's being, so that God remains always divine, even in this process of action.

The discourse about the «God who is in movement» can never omit God's freedom and grace in choosing and loving God's creature, and must count on God's action to save the human being who uses his or her freedom to say «no» to God. For this reason one must speak of God's suffering. Jüngel will say that love necessarily includes passion and suffering. The greatness and divinity of God's love is manifested in God's pain, since God's suffering love leads to victory over death and shows itself to be stronger than death. In the face of the violence and pain which devastates humankind, theology will have to speak of a God capable of suffering and of God's passion, because «God is patient, not in spite of, but on account of being passionate.» Thus one can better understand the creative act of God. Creation is God's act of self-limitation in power and an act of self demotion. In this way a divine coherence is evident between the orders of creation and redemption: both assume a humiliation of God as a free act of love. Therefore the Crucified will always remain the starting point of the concept of the Christian God.

4

God: the Foundation of True Peace

Faith in the God who is love throws light on the search for the peace that humankind is looking for even more anxiously today because it finds itself more threatened. In a world of sin and violence love *cannot* kill and destroy without, at the same time, denying itself as love. Therefore what remains for love is only to suffer and die. Love *can only* suffer, die and resist. Every time justice is violated love suffers. Confronted with the suffering of the innocent, there is no other way for love, no other way for God, except diving into the midst of suffering on the side of the weakest, the oppressed, and suffering with them. Only thus can it be said that love is the ultimate meaning of history, and stronger than death. Only thus can it be said that God is love. Only thus can one understand the relationship between God and evil, between God and the suffering of the world.

God goes to the deepest profundity of suffering and death. God passes through death without being destroyed by it, thus opening up a future of hope and life to all the crucified of history. If we continue, faithful to the tradition of the Church, to hold that God does not come into being, that God does not move and is therefore immutable and impassive, that God is not vulnerable and changeable as the creatures are, we must nevertheless recognize the need to affirm that the heart of God is vulnerable and capable of being affected by the love that opens it to that which is not God, and therefore allows itself to be hurt in its supreme and radical solidarity with suffering humankind.

From the perspective of the Cross of Jesus there is nothing in the world alien to God, nothing which is not assumed (and therefore not redeemed) by God, including negativity, pain and death. However, in spite of this, and in the midst of the struggle against the injustice that continues producing victims, nothing is lost. There is no reason for despair, because redemption exists and proceeds on its mysterious course.

5

Talking About God After September 11, 2001

The thirteenth anniversary of September 11, 2001 —when the world saw itself facing the horror of what happened in New York and Washington with the fall of the twin towers of the World Trade Center, the attack on the Pentagon, and thousands of victims buried under the rubble of the capital of *glamour,* consumption and aesthetic— is certainly one anniversary that the West would not like to celebrate.

Yet neither is what followed that September 11, and continues today, worthy of celebration. After the terrible violence and damage to their country, we saw American troops —in a response that should not have been more than political— sowing retaliation and vengeance on the other side of the world, culminating in the cruel and equivocal Iraq war.

Every day the newspapers showed bleeding photos of Iraqis crying for the loss of one or even all of their family members. The devastated country has been shunted aside, while the big powers prepared new attacks in an effort to make their power ever greater. To an Iraq destroyed and filled with rubble, Ambassador Sérgio Vieira de Mello was sent by the United Nations. He was killed by a suicide attack, another of the thousands of innocent victims of this equivocal and senseless war still being pursued by the great powers.

Furthermore, urban violence continues to produce thousands of victims in the big cities of many countries. In Brazil as many are killed every year as those killed in the Vietnam war. The film by Michael Moore, *Bowling for Columbine,* unveils the true face of American society as a nation dominated by fear, armed to the teeth, fearful of its neighbors and seeing enemies everywhere. So much so that we have already seen even children and teenagers pointing weapons at children they grew up with, as well as killing colleagues and teachers. Or killing in the business of drug trafficking for middle class consumers and falling prey to the unrelenting vicious cycle of violence, from which they can escape only by dying.

Talk of God by the Church and by people of good will must, therefore, be accompanied by endless and tireless peacemaking efforts. In biblical terms the «peaceful» or «peacemaker» is not the same as the «pacifist» —one who, when unjustly injured, is not troubled but remains calm, just trusting God. What is meant is rather an essentially communal or social attitude, a benevolence engaged in building links among the members of a particular society and in restoring those links that unfortunately have been broken. The New Testament shows that this work is above all the work of God, the «God of Peace», whose promise, consummated in Jesus Christ, includes peace in the universe and reconciliation among all people.

The example of those who work for peace is presented in the Gospels as a good venture, as living a life of true happiness. People divided by quarrel are unhappy. One has to lend them a hand, to help them reconcile and rebuild themselves. This attitude of the peaceful and the peacemakers is not merely affective. It is rather an active endeavor that effectively pursues the well being of the other and of the collectivity. Such peacemakers, according to the Gospel, «shall be called the children of God», that is, the «elected». They are elected —whatever situation they find themselves in— to bear a witness whose prototype is Jesus himself, the Son of God and God incarnate.

As for the practice of justice and righteousness on behalf of those who are deprived of this fundamental and vital good, the action by the peacemakers reflects God's mercy for human beings. It is for this reason that the blessedness proclaimed in the Gospel attests that those who build peace shall be called the children of God —because they effectively devote their lives and offer the best of themselves so that peace may reign, restoring ruptured relationships and healing the wounds caused by violence. This is the opposite of the concept of sovereign power that for a long time allowed kings, emperors and all kinds of dictators to proclaim themselves sons of God, as guarantors of peace for their subjects.

Again, the God of our faith shows the true way to end violence. It is not by combating it brutally, which, rather than shrinking it, would make it grow with reprisals and retaliation. Instead, God comes to meet the human being unprotected and disarmed, lovingly offering God's self in a covenantal relationship. The peacemakers are, therefore, those who with courage and lucidity identify the conflict at its roots and assume it from the inside, working with the best of their energies to make possible the restoration of lives devastated by war and barbarity. And they do this aware of the risk of being hit by fragments from the weapons that violence employs to reach its goals.

Conclusion: A Disarmed God

Looking at the God revealed in the pages of Scripture we can perceive a God who is alien to any kind of violence. In God there is no destructive wrath, envy, or vengeance. God is pure nonviolence. Yet the image of a nonviolent God has not always been the dominant one in the readings and interpretations of biblical text. On the contrary, the image of a warrior God takes a central place in the religious archeology of humankind. Those interested in war cannot have any God other than a warrior God. Whom can they beseech for victory, if not the Lord of Hosts? And if we read the Scriptures with care, we will see that human beings are always the ones who beg God to make war. God never begs God's creatures to do such a thing.

Because of this, the representation of God has often remained captive to an archaic religious stereotype of a being who resorts to violence to punish the unfaithful and does not hesitate to make war against the wicked. It is urgent that we give up this stereotype of a severe and violent god and learn about the God who is love and goodness, the God who relates to human beings with pure and freely given compassion and benevolence.

Jesus disarmed God once and for all. More precisely, he disarmed the images of God fabricated by human beings who imagined a God similar to themselves, a God who knocked down all the powerful gods from their thrones. The Lord of Hosts is the truly disarmed God. The power of the all-powerful God shines in the impotence of the love that is rejected and crucified in Jesus Christ. The projection of human frustrations onto divine omnipotence may well turn out to be a projection of the human wish for power.

Since God is pure nonviolence, one can witness God only by becoming a witness to God's nonviolence. The antithesis of faith, in this case, is not unbelief but violence and lovelessness. To deny God is not to ignore God's existence, but to assume that God either accommodates human violence, legitimates it or and directs it.

This disarmed God invites human beings to disarm themselves as well. Only self-disarmament will enable the peacemaker to disarm the adversary. The evangelical blessedness of peace refutes the pagan argument that my adversary's possession of arms justifies me in arming myself to resist him. This attitude can lead only to an arms race to conquer the world, a race that vies for a peace founded only on a balance of terror. The only result of such a race is war.

The pursuit of peace, in opposition to aggression and violence, is the only way to break the rivalry based imitation of the enemy and the vicious circle of endless vengeance. Due to its failure to accept this logic, the history of humankind has become more and more the history of its wars. Only through yearning and action can it become the history of peace built on justice and responsible dialogue.

Now, thirteen years after September 11, the Lord of Hosts threatens to overtake the God of peace, in the belly of the fundamentalist movements that make God combat God's self, in Iraq and elsewhere. The revelation of God the Father, Son and Holy Spirit calls us to speak of God with gentleness and, in God's name, to build a peace without end.

A God who Follows the Rhythm of Life

1

God, Our Servant

I praise you, Lord,
our servant,
in all that is created.

> You orchestrate the song of the cosmos
> and sharpen the listening ear.
> You purify the polluted air
> and open the breathing lung.
> You liquefy the body's blood
> and channel the guiding vein.
> You awaken greenness in the leaf
> and give joy to the gazing eye.

I praise you, Lord,
our servant,
in all that is created.

> You impel us toward others,
> and beguile us from inside other selves.
> You inspire us in constant encounter,
> disclosing yourself afresh each day.
> You bid us serve the people,
> and in their midst it is us you take care of.
> Through love you bestow life on us in every beginning,
> and in love you embrace us at our end.

I praise you, Lord,
our servant,
in all that is created.

In your fondness for us,

in your sleepless presence,

you go from the furrow to the ear of corn

and from bread for the feast;

in the day you wander the streets

and at night you open the door to us;

in the learned you tell us truths

and in the lowliest you impart your very self.

I praise you, Lord,

our servant,

in all that is created.

BENJAMÍN GONZÁLEZ BUELTA, SJ *(p. 155)*

Throughout the course of this journey we have seen that the God of our faith is a mystery, and as such can be neither easily circumscribed by thought nor wholly and satisfactorily expressed by human language.

We could select from many perspectives through which we perceive God in history. We chose two angles of perception that challenge Theology in speaking about belief in God —politics and gender. We all know that politics is an essential dimension of human life. It affects our understanding of God and God's mystery and, for its part, it can and must be affected and transformed by a theology more compatible with the revelation coming from God. As for the issue of gender, it has become one of the most powerful signs of our current times, requiring an inclusive language for the mystery of God— a requirement that both male and female theologians have tried to comply with.

2

The Trinity and Politics

If the Trinitarian matrix critiques and illuminates the entirety of human life, so also politics, as a constitutive feature of the human being and human behavior in the world, should be critiqued and illuminated by it as well. The Trinity and politics are two poles of reflection which will show us that an image of the human being corresponds to an image of God, and that divine praxis must critique and illuminate human praxis, in promoting the common good and the transformation of the world. A Trinitarian theology has a great deal to say about politics —about the human experience of power, participation, and citizenship, as well as about political activity. A Trinitarian theology is critical of, and inspirational for, political experience.

1. The monarchy of the Father: patriarchy or service of fellowship?

The earliest model of Trinitarian theology appeared in the East during the first four centuries, in the context of the growing power of the emperor over society and the Church. It was formulated in the Greek language by the Greek Fathers, among them Origen (c.185-254) and Athanasius (c.296-373), and by the Cappadocian Fathers Basil the Great (c.330-379), Gregory of Nazianzus (c.329-389) and Gregory of Nyssa (c.330-395).

Their *starting point is the person of the Father*. For these theologians God is the Father. Just as described in the Scriptures, God is Yahweh, the liberator of the people of Israel, and the Father of Jesus Christ. According to the suggested order of relationships in the economy of salvation, the Father is not only the first, but also the monarch (from the Greek *monê-archê* = sole principle). The Father is the source, the fountainhead and the origin of everything, the principle of the intra-divine life and therefore of the deity of the Son and the Holy Spirit. As such, the Father is the principle of extra-Trinitarian works, that is, of creation and history. The Father is absolute mystery, inaccessible, the fountainhead that conceals itself while originating life, like a hand that while opening itself to give, also clenches and pulls itself away. The Father is the hidden God, who nevertheless reveals God's self with two hands: the Word (the Son) and the breath that comes with the Word (the Spirit).

This theology aims at preserving the sense of mystery, in which it participates. Thus its concerns are more aesthetic and mystical than ethical and political. It keeps the mystery in the sacred sphere of worship and prayer, of contemplation and adoration. It fears offending the mystery with language that is too daring. It emphasizes the monarchy of the Father, in its theological-Trinitarian sense: in the Trinity there is only one principle and that is the Father, the only center of life from which all things arise. If there were two principles, the movement of the Trinitarian fellowship would come to a halt. But it immediately adds that the monarchy of the Father is neither authoritarian nor all-powerful. Rather than preventing it, the monarchy strengthens the participation of the Son and the Spirit. Both proceed from the Father and participate in the same deity with equal dignity and majesty. The Father exercises this monarchy as a service, and its authority as an agent and the head of the Trinitarian fellowship.

In this way, according to the Trinitarian formulation, adoration is directed to the Father by the Son, in the Spirit, as an acknowledgment that all grace comes from the Father, through the Son, in the Spirit. In this back-and-forth movement, the Father is always found in the beginning and at the pinnacle of the intra-Trinitarian mystery as well as of the salvific history. Here, then, is a theological route that, although starting with the deity of the Father, ends up with the biblical and orthodox faith's clear and explicit affirmation of the deity of each of the three persons in the infinite fellowship of love.

But, alongside the value that this model gives to the mystery and mysticism, to aesthetics and praise, this way of doing theology carries two great dangers to our conception and practice of policy: *patriarchalism* and *spiritualism*. These dangers were not always avoided in the history of Christian theology, pastoral instruction, and Christian policies.

In fact, from the same starting point —the deity of the Father— came the heresy of «subordinationism», which sees the Son and the Holy Spirit as subordinate to the Father. This Trinitarian heresy had two variants: Arianism, from the Alexandrian church elder Arius (c.337), which sees the Son as a demigod or a super-hero, a creature —although a most exalted one— who partakes of God's deity not by nature, but by adoption; and Pneumatomachism (the Greek *pneûma-mackia* = fight against the Spirit), or Macedonian subordinationism, from Bishop Macedonius of Constantinople (c.362), which sees the Holy Spirit as an ether, as the breath of God, who partakes of the deity not by nature, but by emanation.

Thus the preoccupation with salvaging the unique glory of the Father brings the Trinity to an end, in sanctioning the concept of a God, Creator and Lord of the universe, who alone rules over the work of creation, of which the Son and the Spirit are still a part but only as special creatures. The deity of the Son and the Spirit is denied in the interest of saving the Father's monarchy.

These heresies are devoid of the content of the faith which always speaks of three active persons in a single history of salvation, who act interdependently in the history of revelation. Because we believe that in the economy of salvation the real being of God is revealed, we should also believe that there is an interaction in the intimacy of intra-Trinitarian life, among three divine persons who are free and interdependent, without supremacy and subordination —even as we acknowledge, from the perspective of a history of revelation in which it is the Father who sends the Son and the Holy Spirit, an order of relationship by which the Father is the origin of the deity of the other two persons.

The danger becomes evident when this theology is applied to politics. The model carries serious risks. It leads to obvious paternalism and patriarchism. It brings about a «religion of the Father», seen as absolute lord, represented on earth by the Son who, in his turn, is seen as a spiritual or political leader.

In intra-ecclesial relations this «religion» is characterized by its spiritual verticalism, ecclesiastic clericalism, judicialism and triumphalism. The model exerted influence in social and political relations by justifying all the absolutist pretensions of monarchs and despots who throughout the centuries identified themselves as God's representatives. In his critique of this model Moltmann says, «The glory of the triune God is reflected neither in the crowns of the kings nor in the triumph of the conquerors, but in the face of the Crucified, and in the face of the oppressed, of whom he became a brother. He is the only visible model of the invisible God. The glory of the triune God is also reflected in the community of Christ: that of the faithful and the poor».

In this model there is no place for those at the bottom. The king or president of the nation, the principal or teacher in the school, the father in the family, the priest in the parish, etc.—each one at his or her level makes all the decisions that apply to all the others. The laity have no voice in the Church; citizens do not participate in elections; children, youth and women must obey the head of the household; and minorities are repressed. It is only with the advent of modernity that a more practical and democratic conception of exercise of power and social organization has become prevalent.

The model carries still another great danger: spiritualism deprived of reality. Aware that Manichaeism is «the psychological basis of Arianism», J. L. Segundo warns of the danger of spiritualism. Spiritualist Manichaeism, so present in the gnostic movements of our time, including in Christian settings, separates history into two parts and divides the human being into body and spirit. It values only the spiritual and religious dimension, envisaging God only within the limits of the sacred, and making impossible access to the mystery through the mediation of material things and the conflictive nature of history. Following this conception—denying the possibility of a linkage of the human, the material and the biological with the divine— Arianism ended up denying the deity of Jesus as well. Those Christians who seek a God in the highest, a Father without a world, a Christ without praxis, a faith without politics, forget that the mystery hides in history.

Yet, even with the risk of paternalism and patriarchism, and of manichaeism and spiritualism in their ecclesial and cultural variants, this model carries something of great value: the importance of *authority to serve* and the *search for the mystery*. Today there is a growing clamor for authority at the service of coordination and organization as well as for evidence regarding mystery and spirituality. No ecclesial or social organization can survive without the internal dynamics of the exercise of power, and without reference to the transcendent verticality of the mystery. In the Trinity, the power of the Father is exerted as service to the fellowship. The Trinity, according to this first model of theological reflection, challenges all forms of authoritarianism and spiritualism and is an inspiration for life in fellowship, where power is exercised not as a monopoly but as a sharing in which all search for kinship in the encounter with the mystery of the Father (Puebla 241).

2. The essence of the One and only: uniformity or the promise of unity?

The second model appeared in the fourth century in the West, in a time of anxiety about the unity of the Roman empire, then threatened with invasions by people from the North. At the beginning of the second millennium, it was reinforced amid concern for the unity of Europe and Mediaeval Christianity —at a time of the formation of nations as well as of the first signs of their emancipation from ecclesiastic tutelage. This model was formulated in the Latin language by the Latin Church Fathers and the Scholastics, above all by Augustine (c.430) and later by Thomas Aquinas (c.1274).

Its starting point is the question of the essence of the One and Only God. For these theologians the real God is the Trinity, exactly as shown in Scripture: a God who is the communion between Father, Son and Holy Spirit. The intention is to salvage the divine fellowship —the equality of the three persons both in eternity and in extra-Trinitarian activity. To salvage the divine unity they insist on a divine essence which is one and unique. The words essence, substance, nature and being are used interchangeably, to accentuate the existence of the one and only God. They strongly emphasize the Oneness of God, leaving little space for the exposition of the Triune God. Theirs is a philosophical language, notable for metaphysical concepts quite distant from the historical and narrative ideas of the Bible. That makes its access difficult for popular religiosity and spirituality.

To understand and explain the unity of the divine essence, the theologians who propose and follow this model begin with the person of the Father as the eternal begetter of the Son, and conclude with the Holy Spirit as proceeding from the uniting and distinctive love between them. Thus, while unity is preserved, distinctions are prominent as well. The model clearly shows who is who. The Father is the lover, the begetter, the unbegotten, the beginning without beginning. The Son is the begotten, the originated, the beginning that comes from the beginning. The Holy Spirit is the tie of love between the Father and the Son, that is, the Spirit of unity and diversity between them.

To describe fellowship in distinctiveness rationally and objectively, this model emphasizes metaphysics, logic, rationality, distinction, organization, and jurisprudence. The intention appears to be to apprehend the being of the Trinity by fitting it into a mathematical formula or theorem. Quite differently from the eastern model of mysticism and aesthetics, this western model supports a logical and juridical understanding as a tangible way to organize faith.

Alongside its emphasis on logic and jurisprudence, on essence and distinction, on incarnation and organization —all of them so typical of western societies and the western Church— the model carries several great dangers which were not always avoided in the history of Christian theology, pastoral instruction, and Christian policies: *uniformization, institutionalism and rationalism.*

Coming from the same starting point —the unity of God's essence— some heresies of the Third Century focused so much on unity that they ended up rejecting the differences among the three divine persons. Denying that Jesus of Nazareth could be God if he was carnal and mortal, Docetism taught that he was the one and only God in human form. Several other Trinitarian heresies developed under the inspiration of this Christological heresy. Eventually grouped under the name of Modalism, they taught that there is just one God —the One and only God— self-revealed in our history in three modalities: as the Father in the Old Testament, as the Son in Jesus of Nazareth, and as the Holy Spirit in the early Church. The divine persons were seen in their salvific functions, but not in their own individuality and identity. They were seen as roles or masks used at different times by the same (and only) deity.

This preoccupation with salvaging the unity of the essence of God brings the Trinity to an end, as was the case with the previous model. It establishes the conception of the one and only God, Creator and Lord of the Universe, who rules over the work of creation and history, revealing God's self through different masks and roles in their corresponding functions as creator, redeemer and sanctifier. Similarly to the previous model, these heresies are devoid of the biblical content which always refers to three different individuals in a unique fellowship, acting together and interdependently in a unique history of salvation. The history of revelation leads to the understanding that in the intimacy of intra-Trinitarian life there is a dynamic in which the three persons are not simply functions, but entities with their own identities and their own subjectivity. Among themselves they are at once free and interdependent.

The danger in applying this theology to politics is evident. This is less true of the orthodox legacy of Augustine and Thomas Aquinas, and more so of the legacy of docetism and modalism. The latter entails serious risks. The consequences are the same as those of the previous model, aggravated by functionalism, institutionalism and uniformism. It results in a religion of the essence of God, a «religion of the one and only God», seen as the absolute Lord and represented on earth by strong institutions, such as state power, a harmonious society, and the patriarchal family. In this «religion of the one and only God» too much space is given to the person of the Son, in the so-called «christomonism». Since the Son becomes flesh in Jesus of Nazareth, in the incarnation and visibility of God as well as in the reconciliation and recapitulation of all things in God, he occupies the central place in this «religion», which could also be known as the «religion of the Son». This christomonism is highly criticized in the history of the Church and theology as responsible for the Western Church's obvious judicialism and rigid clerical uniformity.

Besides the deviations of the previous model, in intra-ecclesial relations this «religion» is characterized by its liturgical ritualism, moralistic jurisprudence, ecclesiastic institutionalism and bureaucratic functionialism. The model also had an influence on social and political relations, in justifying all efforts toward the uniformization of state and social institutions.

In the Church, as in society, what mattered was not people but institutions. People should fulfill their functions in an orderly way or be excluded, in the interests of preserving the institution. To protect the power and sovereignty of the institution, any opposition was silenced. The institutions of family, school, and parish, among others, prevailed over liberty and conscience as well as over the dignity and responsibility of their members. There was no place in the Church for a diversity of gifts, vocations, communities and movements. There was no place in society for a variety of organizations, associations, parties and groups. There was no place in the family and the school for the expression of the concerns of women, youth, and students. In this Eurocentric culture there was no place for indigenous people or people of color. The defense of unity degenerated into uniformity. Uniformity prevailed.

To these dangers one must add the theological rationalism that contrived to master God with the idea of the natural God, an entity completely incompatible with the Christian God. It is a product of rational reductionism, ancient modalism and modern atheism —and certainly not disinterested in politics.

Observing the strong presence of this concept of God in theology, J. L. Segundo denounced it as follows: «In this nature [theology] sees only that which can be deduced from its infinitude, from its absolute sufficiency and from its all-encompassing value, identified with a happiness without darkness or fear. This nature, considered nothing less than God, separates him in an abysmal and irreversible way from all created nature and, because of this, from all change, all pain and all history». Christians who look for a God outside of the world and outside of history, alien to social changes and conflicts —those who live by a static faith, without politics— forget that the God of Israel and Jesus Christ is «a God who, although not needing, by his own nature, to suffer, change, and die, yet loved freely, and surrendered himself, in every sense of the word, to the logic of this love».

Criticizing this model from the standpoint of the Trinitarian doctrine of the realm of freedom, Moltmann writes: «Monarchic monotheism legitimates the Church as a hierarchy, as a sacred power... The Trinitarian doctrine (on the contrary) constitutes the Church as a community without domination... Instead of authority and obedience, primacy is given to dialogue, consensus and harmony... Instead of hierarchy, which preserves and imposes unity, the fraternity of brothers and sisters appears in the fellowship of Christ». This critique of the model's influence in the life of the Church certainly applies as well to its historical and cultural leverage in society. Indeed, it was only with the advent of modernity that a more democratic conception of institutions —and more democratic practices— became prevalent.

But while it is true that this model entails the risks of uniformization and institutionalism, as well as of rationalist abstraction and theist dualism, it is also true that it poses the question of unity. The model carries something of great value: *holistic integration*. The modern and postmodern world is fragmented. It has lost the stability and security offered by the unity of medieval Christianity, built on the Latin model: only one Church —the catholic; only one race—

the white race; only one continent —Europe; only one conceptual matrix—God's created nature, etc. A diversity of situations, ideas and values is characteristic of the modern and postmodern world. All this matters, as we will see. Yet the eagerness for diversity and pluralism can degenerate into splintering and disintegration. As much as they value pluralism, human beings have not abandoned their yearning for unity. There are several national and worldwide religious and social phenomena and expressions that point precisely to the promise of holism, the integration of the human being with God and the cosmos, and unity among cultures and religions.

The Trinity, in the conception of this second model of theological reflection, represents a critique of all forms of universalization, institutionalization and rationalism that annihilate differences. But it also represents an inspiration for a striving towards unity as well as for the appreciation and work of ecclesial fellowship and social organization.

3. The distinctions among the Three: anarchy or democratic participation?

The third model is still in its phase of germination and development. It emerges from the human yearning for liberty and equality, individuality and participation. Theologians from the most distinguished Christian traditions are working on it.

The starting point of the model is the distinctiveness of the divine persons. The Biblical revelation speaks of three divine subjects who reveal themselves mutually and act interdependently in the history of salvation. This perspective leads to the understanding that in the intimacy of Trinitarian life there may also be a fellowship in which the difference, identity and propriety of each one of the three are taken into account. The fellowship neither eliminates nor promotes these distinctions. It exists precisely for the sake of —and as mediator of— the diversity of the three. The Trinity is not an anonymous society —it is not a mix of beings without personality. On the contrary, it is a fellowship of distinct persons, each one with particular characteristics. The Father is paternal, creative and life-giving. The Son is receptive and welcoming. The Spirit is diversifying in unity and unifying in diversity. Although very different, they are not divided and separate. They are fully interdependent, as in the so called perichoretic fellowship, that is, in the mutual inter-penetration of the three persons.

With the objective of showing how personal differences realize and animate fellowship, this model emphasizes diversity, participation, subjectivity, individuality, freedom and conscience. It differs significantly from the previous models in emphasizing the participatory, egalitarian, libertarian and democratic orientation to life and faith.

While valuing participation, democracy, subjectivity, brotherhood and sisterhood, this model also entails great dangers, such as *anarchy, division and individualism*, which were not always avoided in the history of theology, pastoral instruction and Christian policies. In their concern to salvage the distinctiveness of God, some heresies of earlier centuries (like that of Bishop Dionysius of Alexandria in the mid-Third Century, reacting to Sabellianism) fell into a tritheism that enabled a contradictory vision of the Trinity as including three gods and three distinct principles of being. In the Thirteenth Century, the Trinitarian theology of Abbot Joachim de Fiore (1135-1202) was questioned by the Lateran Council IV (1215). Fiore identified the three persons with three presumed eras of history (the Father with the Old Testament and an era of slavery, the Son with the New Testament and an era of grace, the Holy Spirit with an era of liberty and yearnings for renewal). He separated the three persons and provided no clear explanation of the real and eternal fellowship among them. This way of thinking runs the risk of dividing the Trinity and obliterating the unity and oneness of God.

The preoccupation with salvaging the differences curtails fellowship and promotes a conception of a God divided into isolated entities. As in the case of the previous models, these heresies —or at least ambiguities— are devoid of the content of the revelation which always points to three different subjects in a unique fellowship. The history of salvation leads to the conclusion that in the intimacy of the intra-Trinitarian life there is a dynamic of life and fellowship in which the three persons are divided and separate. They are realities with their own identities and subjectivity, free and independent among themselves, while living in an eternal fellowship grounded in, and mediated by, their differences.

The danger that arises in applying this theology to politics is evident. The consequences —subjectivism, anarchy, democratism, basism, conflictivism, and sectorialism[1]— are very different from those of the previous models. A «religion of the Spirit» emerges without any criteria of identity and differentiation for access to God. This «religion» could work out in two ways. One way is for each group

---

1 *Translator's note:* No adequate translation was found for «basism» (basismo), «sectorialism» (setorialismo), or «assemblism» (assembleísmo) that is why we explain the sense of the terms: Basismo: to consider as true only that which comes from below, from the grassroots, the «basis». Setorialismo: that considers only a sector and of reality and not the whole. Assembleísmo: comes from the assemblies, the gatherings of the basic communities. Everything that was approved there was accepted without being criticized or questioned.

to create its own God —the God of each culture, religion, church, movement and community— generating moral relativism, social conflict and religious apathy. The other way is to create the impersonal God of the New Era —the God of the amorphous conciliation of all ideas and values, even if contradictory among themselves.

In intra-ecclesial relations this religion is characterized by sectorialism in pastoral instruction, by basism in the communities, and by anarchy in the celebrations. In social and political relations, one finds assemblism[2] in the councils, and democratism in the relations.

This model, unlike the previous one, does not give as much weight to institutions as to persons. It values plurality as much in Church as in society, often to the detriment of unity. Institutions are criticized as superstructures ideologically produced by economic and political interests. This criticism follows two lines. The liberal (now neo-liberal) capitalist line, with a functionalist interest in institutions, criticizes them for being too much under state control and therefore failing to leave space for individual freedom and private initiative. The Marxist collectivist line criticizes them, with dialectic emphasis, for exploiting and oppressing enormous numbers of low paid working people who are excluded from the means and benefits of production. Yet both critiques, based on either religious monotheism or atheistic pantheism, promote the creation of an inhumane society. Capitalism is selfish, and socialism leads to collectivization and cultural homogenization.

As stated by Moltmann, «Western personalism has to this day partnered with monotheism, while Eastern socialism has, from a religious perspective, a pantheistic rather than an atheistic basis.» And he concludes, «For this reason Western personalism and Eastern socialism have not been reconciled to this day. Individual human rights and social rights appear separate from each other. The Trinitarian Christian doctrine could play an important role in achieving the necessary convergence toward a truly humane society».

This model has the advantage of being able to influence church and society in justifying any intention to democratize organizations and institutions. It carries something of great value: *ecclesial fellowship and participatory democracy.*

More time and, above all, more practice of democratic policy, more fellowshipping and ecclesial participation, and more practice of community power will be needed to strengthen the arguments of this third model. We are living out a unique moment in the history of the faith. Throughout the first centuries of Christianity, the Church received the Gospel from a Judaic culture still immersed

2 See note 1.

in a Greco-Roman environment. Now it is time for its acculturation into a post-modern, urban and global environment. The emerging new model of Trinitarian theology may not be able to put its mark on the social and ecclesial relations of our time. But this model will be determinative for the survival of the Church and of humankind in approaching times! Dependent on the strength of this model are the freedom movements of the poor, of indigenous peoples, of people of color, of children and women, of oppressed cultures and religions, and the movement for religious plurality now yearning for dialogue.

Proposed by Moltmann as the Trinitarian doctrine of the Kingdom of God and human freedom, this model emphasizes the contribution of each divine person (creation as the work of the Father, redemption as the work of the Son, and glorification as the work of the Spirit) for the edification of the Kingdom of God and as the foundation for the freedom of each human being and all humankind. Surpassing the old method of domination, he submits fellowship. «While freedom is a simple domain, in order to be able to dominate one must separate, isolate, individualize and differentiate. But if freedom means fellowship or community, then one must live out the unification of all separated things... Freedom as fellowship is, therefore, the movement opposite to the history of struggles for power and of class struggles».

As we conclude this reflection about the Trinity and politics, we are aware that each Trinitarian theological model brings assets and risks to the exercise of political and ecclesial power. For this reason one should avoid falling into the idealistic choice of one single model to the exclusion of the others, and simply transplanting it, disregarding the historical and cultural factors that have brought the three of them. It is necessary to take advantage of the contributions of each one, while establishing criteria that may neutralize the implied dangers that they carry.

Knowing that the first model favors the biblical basis of the order of relations, that the second favors fellowship, and that the third favors distinctions, one can expect that in an inclusive integration of the three, the contribution of one model will prevent the other two from leading to either heresies or inhumane and unjust political practices. The first model, in emphasizing authority, will prevent society and the Church from becoming amorphous and anarchical. The second, with its emphasis on fellowship, will prevent authoritarianism and individualism. The third, in valuing differences, will prevent oppression and cultural homogenization.

The third model, which is still being shaped even today, can only flourish if the communal and participatory exercise of power is practiced in interpersonal, group and community relations. It is urgent to strengthen the relationship between a Trinitarian theology based on the distinctiveness of the divine persons on the one hand, and a political and pastoral practice that takes into account the diversity of persons, situations, gifts and ministries, on the other.

In the communal and participatory practice of power, both ecclesial and social, there will certainly be an order of relations with a clearly transparent exercise of authority. The first model is pertinent. However, authority will be exercised on the basis of an awareness of the possession of adequate gifts. Such gifts are received from the Spirit and ratified by the community.

In the second model, with its emphasis on institutions and the distribution of roles and functions, the Church as well as society can survive only with organization. Yet the institutional and organizational structure will only make sense if it serves to support the dynamics of life and the diversity of gifts. Therefore the institution itself will be subject to the questioning of the Spirit.

Be that as it may, the challenges of the modern and postmodern world demand that we present ourselves to the humankind of the third millennium with a renewed image of God's mystery, namely, one that justifies and upholds a new proposal for social organization and political practice. The third model addresses these challenges.

The God of our faith can no longer act as an alibi for colonial imperialism, oppressive machismo and marginalist exclusivism. God can no longer be presented as an idol. God must shine differently from the gods of modernity, those idols that demand the sacrifice of the poor in order to stay in power. As the source of all power, the God of the Christian faith will use it in self-dispossession and humility, decisively confirming what is shown to us in the praxis of Jesus of Nazareth.

3
The Trinity from the Perspective of Gender

The second angle through which we'll observe the Trinitarian mystery is feminism, the sign of the times that so greatly challenges Christianity and our theological language. How do we speak of God in a feminine way? How do we surmount the machista language about God and each one of the divine persons? Is this possible? Based on what criteria? In our view feminine language is not only useful and necessary but also enriching for theology, and not only convenient but also convincing. It helps us to better know even the deepest mystery of our Trinity-God.

Let us draw our attention to each one of the divine persons and their feminine characteristics. We will emphasize what we can perceive of the mystery of divine love and of the means of God's salvific actions among us. The contemplation of this Revelation of the Incarnate Son and of the Spirit, which labors in the womb of history, will allow us to arrive at the Origin without origin, which leads us to the ineffable mystery of the internal life of God, the Father of all parenthood.

1. *In the Son, God made God's self flesh of man and woman.* From the Gospel narrative one learns that the historical Jesus initiated a charismatic itinerant movement in which men and women acted together as fellow workers. This differed from the movement started by John the Baptist, who emphasized asceticism and penance, and from the Qumrān movement which admitted only men.

Besides proclaiming the Kingdom, the movement of Jesus was characterized by joy and the absence of prejudice (all kinds of sinners and marginalized persons were welcome at meals and celebrations), and by the dismissal of many of the enduring taboos of the society of the time. His disregard of taboos related to women was one of the most significant examples.

Jesus's attitude toward women was considered uncommon at the time, even for his disciples (Jn. 4:27). The idea that women are part of, and active participants in, the Kingdom (Lk. 10: 38-42) as well as privileged beneficiaries of the Master's miracles, is found in all four Gospels (Lk. 8:2, Mk. 1:29-31, 5:25-34, 7:24-30 and others).

Jesus's attitude toward women has theological meaning for us today. For one thing, it highlights a most important aspect of the Gospel: the Good News announced to the poor. Jesus wanted to free the disinherited and the rejected, the sinners, the heathen and all who are marginalized, including women and children, who were not considered important in Jewish society. He gave them privileged places in his Kingdom. He integrated them into the community of God's children. In them Jesus recognized the precious life of the trampled reed or the still smoking wick.

In accepting women as they were —which included their bodies, then considered weak and impure by his own culture— Jesus sanctions an integrated anthropology that sees the human being as a mix of body and spirit (cf. Mt. 9:20-22, 9:18-19, Lk. 7:36-50).

Having analyzed the attitude of Jesus toward women, we must now consider the feminine in Jesus. It is a given in modern psychology that every human being is, in different proportions, both masculine and feminine. If this idea —nowadays widely accepted— is true, then Jesus, who was a male person, had a feminine dimension as well. Jesus supercedes the androcentrism of his time and integrates into himself so many characteristics of feminine and masculine behavior that we can consider him the first fully mature human person, perfectly integrated into his masculinity and femininity.

The gospels portray Jesus as a man who was not ashamed of his own feelings. And we dare to say that in the deepest of his being Jesus felt the emotion and pain that afflicted the *rachamin* of Yahweh in the Old Testament. We see this emotion in Jesus when he weeps for his dead friend Lazarus (Jn. 11:35), when he laments over the city which will be considered responsible for his martyrdom (Lk. 19:41), and when he weeps over the «baby chicks» of Jerusalem whom he wished he could shelter under his wings (Lk. 13:34).

There is one woman in particular who helps us to better understand the mystery of the feminine in the Son of God. The Son of the Father who pre-exists all eternity and who gave us the power to be God's children and to call God our Father, is also born of a woman (cf. Gal. 2:4) —he the son of Mary (cf. Mk. 6:3, Mt. 13:55, Jn. 6:42). This is the process of kenotic descent, of incarnation, exalted by the Letter to the Phillippians (2:5-8). Therefore this Son is in no way different from the one who was born of Mary's flesh and shocked his contemporaries, who, upon seeing his performance of powerful signs and wonders, said: «Is not this the carpenter, the son of Mary...?» (Mk. 6:3, see also Mt. 13:35, Jn. 6:42).

The New Testament places the man and the woman, Jesus and Mary, at the center of the mystery of the incarnation, a mystery that is the salvation of all humankind. God assumes human flesh in and by woman, and is «born of a woman». God did not become human to be identified with only half of humankind. God became flesh —flesh of man and woman— so that the way to the Father would pass through the masculine as well as the feminine human condition.

The mystery of the incarnation of Jesus in the flesh of Mary teaches us that the human person is not divided into a body of sin and imperfection and a spirit of greatness and transcendence. It is in the debility, in the poverty and in the limitations of human flesh —the flesh of man and woman— that the ineffable greatness of the Spirit can be contemplated and adored.

2. The Spirit is innate maternal love. The Spirit has in the Old Testament the basic meaning of wind. The term *ruach* is almost always feminine. With a few exceptions and connotations the *ruach* is the presence of the real God, who gives birth to life in movement and otherness.

From the innermost center of divine identity —of the *ruach*— the Divine Spirit induces from chaos the birth of the cosmos. The *ruach* is the divine way through which the divine contractions of the Creator Father make possible the existence of the universe. This same *ruach*, mother and source of life, takes things from where they are not so that they may be. She installs in the heart of reality the fundamental difference between creation and Creator, thus laying the basis for what will be the dialogue of covenant and love. It is she who will take possession of the prophets, inspiring them to speak the words of life whispered in their ears by Yahweh (cf. Ezek. 36 & 37, 1 Sam. 10:6-10, 2 Kings 3:15ff). In more recent texts she is identified with God (Isa. 63:10-11, Ps. 51:13), laying the basis for what will appear in the New Testament as the Third Person of the Trinity—the Holy Spirit, who comes as a dove upon Jesus at the Jordan River (Mk. 1:9-11) and who is called, with feminine accents, a Comforter, the artisan of the new creation.

In the New Testament the Holy Spirit appears and is perceived in the community as an «other» who brings protection and comfort during the absence of the Son. Scripture tells us that in the absence of Jesus the Spirit takes his place in the community of faith, as «another Paraclete», who lives among us at the side of the baptized as their defender and comforter.

The Spirit supports and brings comfort as well as an opening to otherness. During the absence of the Son, the Spirit remains in the community of the baptized as their defender and comforter. Being neither the Father nor the Son, the Spirit can be identified as the «other» who appears and begins to be, par excellence, the divine «presence» in a world that weeps for and laments the absence of the Savior, and feels insecure and threatened with a return to primeval chaos.

Some references to the Spirit by Jesus in the Gospel of John have maternal connotations. The Spirit will not leave us orphaned (Jn. 14:18); the Spirit comforts us and counsels us like a loving mother (14:26). Paul speaks of the Spirit doing things that are usually done by a mother, such as teaching us to babble the names of the Abba-father (Rom. 8:15) and of Jesus Christ as Lord (1 Cor. 12:3), as well as teaching us to ask in a way that is acceptable and pleasant to God (Rom. 8:26).

Mary's virginal conception is the work of the Father, and we can affirm as well that this work of the Father is received by the Holy Spirit. It is a Maternal Love, a conceiving Love, a fertile divine receptivity that impregnates a virgin, thus making divinely possible what is humanly impossible. It changes the logical direction of reality and inaugurates a totally other logic, and, in the untouched difference of the woman Mary of Nazareth, it allows the birth of an even deeper difference: the Incarnate Word, God made flesh in the womb of humankind.

While it is a delicate matter to affirm that the Holy Spirit is the Divine Mother of the man Jesus of Nazareth, one can say without a shadow of doubt that the Holy Spirit, the *ruach* of the Old Testament and the *pneuma* in the New Testament, is the divine-maternal love of the Father in the human conception of Christ.

3. *The Son and the Holy Spirit lead to the invisible Father,* the Abba of eternal love, the Beginning without beginning, the Mystery without end. This mystery is the most excellent expression of the paternity that Jesus named as Abba-Father! Can theology, whether in joy (Mt. 11:25-27), in anxiety (Mk. 14:32-42), or in solemn devotion (Jn. 17:11ff), find in this Father any feminine or maternal characteristics? Would the Father of Jesus, the great mystery of the Christian faith, allow us to find feminine and maternal aspects in his person?

God the Father is, above all, the Father of Jesus Christ. Only the relationship of Jesus with the Father can be the key to the interpretation of God's paternity. Is the Father, whom many believers claim to worship, indeed solitary, invulnerable and impassive? Our answer is no, because such characteristics are far from the biblical idea of God. As we have already seen, the God of the Bible, who is the powerful Lord, the fearful Warrior, and the Creator of all that exists, is at the same time a God of clemency and tenderness, whose mercy (*chesed*) never fails from generation to generation. The deepest profundities of this God of clemency are compared to a womb (*rachamim*) moved by compassion for the beloved Son.

This God with a womb is the Father of our Lord Jesus Christ. This is the Father who, as Mystery of the Beginning without beginning and Source of Life, cannot be Father only, but must be both Father and Mother.

If the Son comes from the Father only, then this eternally engendered event must be considered gestation and birth. There is here a significant change in the understanding of the Father. A father that begets a son and brings him into the world cannot be simply a father. He must be a maternal father. Thus God is both the maternal father of God's only begotten Son and also the paternal Mother of the son given birth by God.

The Church affirms this in the Council of Toledo XI, in 675: «...we must believe that the Son did not come from nothing, nor from any other substance, but was engendered or born (*genitus vel natus*) "from the Father's womb" (*da utero Patris*)».

Here, without recourse to patriarchal categories, the wisdom of the Church went beyond patriarchal monotheism and matriarchal pantheism, thus avoiding any dualism between earth and heaven. The Christian Trinitarian doctrine, with its affirmations about the mystery of Jesus's Abba Father as maternal Father and paternal Mother, opens the way for the formation of a community of men and women who, «in the unity of the Holy Spirit» (2 Cor. 13:13), should supercede privilege and domination of any kind.

The maternal Father of Jesus also allows us to go beyond the dualism of body and soul. The patriarchal God is distant and sovereign, invulnerable to the pain and suffering of humankind, and silent before the Cross of the Son whom He supports in history. In contrast, the Abba of Jesus —the Mystery of life that conceives and gives birth— deeply participates in, and lovingly partakes of, the sufferings of the people of Israel. This God lives among the humble and accompanies the children of Jacob even into their exile.

In the passion of the Son, the Father achieves the greatest loving universal opening. In delivering the beloved Son, conceived and born of God, into the hands of men, the Abba is also delivered —and suffers, in his divine womb as maternal Father, the infinite pain of anguished impotence in the death of his maternal paternity which was crucified on the Cross of the Son for all eternity. However, at the same time and in the same unequaled dynamic of Trinitarian love, the passion of this God who is the maternal Father, who is the Son, who is the Spirit of love, opens wide the gates of salvation to all the abandoned of this world.

Our liberation from pain and suffering finds its source in the suffering of the Trinity: in the death of the Son, in the pain of the Father and in the patient resilience of the Spirit. God makes us free to live in compassionate love.

In the passion of the Son, the maternal Father and the Spirit of Love join with those who must learn, by living and suffering, to be humans in a community grounded in *agape*. There is, in the passion of Trinitarian love, a full integration and redemption of all dimensions of the human being. The disappearance of patriarchal structures implies a real revolution which affects all human language about God. It is the deepest change of paradigm ever seen in the history of Christian doctrine.

As for anthropology and the concept of God, the divine image is found as much in women and as in men. If the God we believe in reveals both male and female characteristics and behaviors, then from now on we will have to describe God using both feminine and masculine words, metaphors and images. If women as well as men are theomorphic —made in the image of God— then it is imperative that this God, of whom both are the image, not be described or thought of as simply andromorphic, but rather as anthropomorphic. We know we will have to struggle with the poverty of human language in its limited ability to express the majesty and ineffability of the divine. For the time being, we will try to combine two symbols, two languages, and two metaphors —masculine and feminine— to achieve a better description of the divine.

The crisis of masculinity, of the father, results not so much from the loss of patriarchal power in society and an antagonistic as well as «demanding and always self assured female», as it does from a culture that has humiliated the male, accusing him of being rough and vulgar while trivializing his phallus, his virility, and his own capacity to give and generate life.

The true father can only go beyond the crisis of his own paternity, and of paternity in general, by renouncing possession of what he has fathered, and by consenting to be only its guardian and provider of love. The human father and mother must also be persons capable of eliciting faithfulness as the ground for a human existence aiming at a higher destiny and higher attributes.

Rather than killing the father, our faith teaches us that he must rise from numerous deaths —some of them necessary— in his symbolic and social history. Besides being coordinates in our everyday life, death and resurrection are also two cardinal concepts of our culture coming from its Hebrew-Christian matrix. The current generation is called to follow a cultural way that is the opposite of the one that caused the theoretical —and lately the social— dismantling of paternity. Today's Christians are called —as in the famous gospel story of the prodigal son— to get up and walk once again to meet the father. There they will find a Father with a deeply maternal and compassionate womb and open arms, ready to receive them with celebration, joy and boundless love.

I Believe in a God Whose Face is Love

Not a God Alone

«God alone is enough»,
but a God
for whom being alone
in all the universe
is not enough.

God draws near to us
in every being in the world
which is
home, nourishment,
undertaking and horizon.
Cosmic communion
which makes us one with God
in the life that fills us
through the senses,
his gift and presence
in us beyond measure!

Our God,
in the communion
that takes shape in all,
with neither rest nor anything to spare,
in the mothering womb
of breathless history.

God free and unique
in the innermost nook
of hushed intimacy,
where every person
becomes coherent.

Eclipsed God,
of whom all we can hang on to
are his traces,
as frail as the breath
of a marginal child
or as mighty as an earthquake
ripping asunder soul
and empires.

Face-to-face God,
transfigured
in an instant,
when everything else
is lit up from within
in its truth
or vanishes
in appearance.

«God alone is enough»,
but a God
for whom being alone
in all the universe
is not enough.

BENJAMÍN GONZÁLEZ BUELTA, SJ *(p. 158)*

We have tried throughout this book to catch a glimpse of some traits of the God
of our faith. We made some approximations to that goal, while aware of the fact
that all our poor attempts may turn out to be spare and insufficient. Ours has
been a dialogue with the Greater Mystery that since the origin of times has at-
tracted and fascinated humankind.

The people of the Bible had the right intuition —that nobody could see the
face of God and stay alive. Also, the approach to the revelation of the divine face
neither is, nor can be, an abstract speculation for official theologians only. It is,
rather, the revelation of the Greater Mystery of Love, a return to that Center
which is the Love of God. This is the only way to bring to the human being an

understanding of the meaning of life, of the liberation of the world and of history, as well as of the salvation of humankind.

We hope we have shown, in the course of this journey, that the persistence of gestures, signs and words that configure the whole Christian experience and praxis IN THE NAME OF THE FATHER, THE SON AND THE HOLY SPIRIT is still meaningful. This is not a matter of affirming the priority of experience over praxis or of praxis over experience, or even of claiming that knowledge takes priority over both, and could survive without either one of them. It is rather a matter of recognizing that a dialectic exists among these three poles: *experience, praxis and the knowledge of God*. It follows that the face of God allows itself to be perceived or discerned only when these three poles are merged in the search for it, in its acknowledgment and in the announcement of it. If that were not the case we would have to do without the Revelation itself, and without meditation, prayer and spirituality, in dealing with faith and theology.

The result of such an omission would be an emptiness in the experience of the mystery of the Trinitarian God, and a multiplication of either integrist and verticalist movements (religion of the Father only), horizontalist and reductionist movements (religion of the Son only), or charismatic and Pentecostal movements (religion of the Spirit only), disconnected from a profound and real experience of the God of the People of Israel, of the God of Jesus and of God's message.

The surmounting of the false ideas about God therefore happens not through ideological confrontations, but through an encounter with the revealing figure of Jesus Christ and the subversive experience of His Spirit. It also comes about through the vital experience of worshiping, following, and being moved by a God who is an infinite fellowship of love and solidarity.

Theology, in itself, is not *the* revelation, but rather a contingent and limited image of it. Only the *Kyrios* (the glorified Lord) has a holistic and global vision of revelation. Thus, every revelation must be critiqued and judged by the figure of Jesus Christ, in revelation, contemplation, and discipleship, and by the divine Breath of the Spirit who proceeds from the Father and the Son in creation, in history, in the Church, and in each human being. The human discourse about God, therefore, must be constantly judged by the Word of God. Only through revelation by this word can the finite and contingent human being endeavor to approach the ineffable and resplendent face of the God who is wholly Other, and who reveals God's self in history while building loving relationships with humankind.

Christianity is this new way which fully «un-veils» itself only in the revelation of the mystery of Trinitarian love—the love of God in Jesus Christ—and in the Spirit of God poured over the Church, over history, and over the creation. There, and only there, can the experience of faith and its consequences—evangelization, teaching and theology—find their center.

The pedagogy of faith is, therefore, called to learn from the divine pedagogy of revelation as recorded in the Scriptures. The mystery of the God whom no one has ever seen presents itself, surprisingly, in the historical self-communication of God with the human being. Jesus Christ is the happy synthesis of the revelation of this mystery, being, as he is, God's revelation and humankind's salvation.

For this mystagogy—this pedagogic way— to be carried out, the God whose face has been sought by the human being since the dawn of time cannot be introduced through cold and rational speculation. This God must be introduced by remembering the acts of God on behalf of God's people, from which the people learned of God's face; and by remembering the life of the historical Jesus in contemplation and in discipleship, which, by the grace of the indwelling Sprit, allowed the Christian to live out the experience of the one and triune God. And this must take place without speculative formulation of the doctrine of the Trinity in the terminology invented by the Church during the early centuries of Christianity, such as hypostasis, nature, perichoresis, and procession.

One must confess faith not in a generic God, not in the God of theism, but in God the Father, the Son and the Holy Spirit, with simple New Testament formulations regarding God's concrete existence. In other words, one needs to recite the CREDO without exaggerating either the historical dimension of the New Testament or the speculative and rational dimensions of later dogmatic formulations. Otherwise, the nefarious consequence would be to put aside the Easter faith, the only really important thing in humankind's seeking and finding of the mystery of God.

It is, therefore, important not to separate the historical Jesus from the glorified Lord, but to recognize in the glorified Lord the traits of the man Jesus of Nazareth. And this is something that is made possible only by the Spirit and in the Spirit. In other words, this is tantamount to confessing that *the word continues, by virtue of the resurrection of Jesus, to have a human face.* There is, therefore, a complementarity between the knowledge of Jesus and the knowledge of the mystery of the Trinitarian love, that is, the mystery of God.

To speak in a Christian way, therefore, is to speak *in the name of the Father, the Son, and the Holy Spirit*, understood as the self-communication of God with the human being, in history, through the mediation of Jesus Christ and in the gift of the Holy Spirit —that is, as the Immanent Trinity (God in God's self) as self-manifested just as it is in the Economic Trinity (God in God's salvific and loving acts).

In speaking about God in the communication of faith through the gospel, Christian education and theology, one must be faithful to the original precepts of the Holy Scripture as both the starting point and the end point. There, and only there, one finds evidence that Jesus Christ is the exegesis (or interpretation) of the Father, making the apprehension of this Father possible for us (cf. John 1:18). Similarly, the Holy Spirit is for us the exegete, the interpreter and the original theologian of the Son and the Father (John 16:12-15). One cannot comprehend anything about any of the persons without being in the divine fellowship where the three of them «speak» and reveal themselves as the one and only God.

All this shows that we can neither fear the ineffability of the Mystery nor try to fit it into our poor and limited human categories. We are called to embrace and worship it, recognizing that there is something inexplicable to our ears and to our merely human understanding, in the Trinitarian relationship between the Father and the Son, as well as in the intra-Trinitarian relationship among the Spirit, the Father and the Son.

This surmounting of the inherent incomprehensibility of the mystery takes place in the experience of the one and triune God in Jesus Christ, through his relationship with the Father, in the Spirit, for the salvation of the world. And the revelation of this one and triune God takes place in history. The salvation, redemption and liberation of history thus bring about a new creature, a new human being, a new covenant, and a new world.

For the modern and contemporary —often reductionist— humanism, human freedom and submission to the will of God are the irreconcilable poles of an impossible dialectic. In Christianity, on the contrary, the more human beings grow in freedom the more they grow in voluntary and loving unity with the absolute freedom of God, who never ceases to reveal God's self in love.

As we look to Jesus we see God's will, the will of the Word made flesh, the supreme model of human freedom which is only realized in Love. Similarly, the Spirit leads only —and can only lead— to Love. Both the Son and the Spirit lead to the original Love from which all things come: the Father, source of all holiness and all life, whose face reveals itself in the bosom of history as provident, affectionate and caring Love.

The revelation of God in history implies the naming of:

The Father—the origin, without beginning, of the history of human freedom;

The Son—God with us, companion in the historic human adventure, who reveals in history what God is for the human being and what the human being is for God. He is the definitive in history and, at the same time, a «new beginning»;

The Spirit—the supreme freedom of Love in the interior of the human being, making possible a response by faith as well as the language of faith (theology), re-creating freedom in Love, and re-directing history toward its eschatological goal.

In Christianity the knowledge of God comes, therefore, from a divine process of restoration of meaning to a history violated by sin, and can only emerge when linked to a concrete historical project to transform human relationships also distorted by sin. This is the Church's reason for being. The experience of God mediated by Jesus Christ in the Holy Spirit —who guides the ecclesial community and opens all of creation to love— is the only force able to bring about the ascension of humankind to a new earth.

The Trinitarian God, the Christian concept of God, at once is and is not Judaic or Greek. It is, above all, revealed. It pertains to the biblical God, the God of Israel and Jesus Christ. To confess that «God exists» means, therefore, to confess that «this» God, the Triune God —Father, Son and Holy Spirit— exists. It is to confess that the face of this same God, whom no one has seen and remained alive, has been made accessible as the Holy Mystery of Love. And we can say that Love is the ultimate meaning of history, and that there is no reality, no matter how negative, that can cause history to descend into the abyss of incomprehensibility and into the darkness of the absurd.

Bibliography

BINGEMER, M. C. L. *Alteridade e vulnerabilidade. Experiência de Deus e pluralismo religioso no moderno em crise.* São Paulo, Loyola, 1993.

BOFF, L. *A Trindade e a Sociedade.* Petrópolis, Vozes, 1988.

_____. *A Santíssima Trindade é a melhor comunidade.* Petrópolis, Vozes, 1988.

BOURGEOIS, H. *Deus segundo os cristãos.* São Paulo. Paulinas, 1977.

CARAVIAS, J. L. *O Deus de Jesus.* Petrópolis, Vozes, 1987.

CATÃO, F. *A Trindade. Uma aventura teológica.* São Paulo, Paulinas, 2000.

CODINA, V. *Creio no Espírito Santo. Ensaio de pneumatologia narrativa.* São Paulo, Loyola, 1997.

COMBLIN, J. *O Espírito Santo e a libertação.* Petrópolis, Vozes, 1987.

DURRWELL, F. *El Espiritu Santo en la Iglesia.* Salamanca, Sígueme, 1986.

_____. *O Pai. Deus em seu mistério.* São Paulo, Paulinas, 1990.

FORTE, B. *Jesus de Nazaré, história de Deus, Deus da história. Ensaio de uma cristologia como história.* São Paulo, Paulus, 1987.

_____. *A Trindade como história.* São Paulo, Paulus, 1987.

GONZÁLEZ BUELTA SJ, BENJAMÍN. *Psalms to accompany the Spiritual Exercises of St Ignatius of Loyola.* Translated by Damian Howard S.J. The Way, Oxford 2012.

GOPEGUI, J. A. R. *de Conhecimento de Deus e evangelização. Estudo teológico-pastoral em face da prática evangelizadora da America Latina.* São Paulo, Loyola, 1977.

GUTIÉRREZ, G. *O Deus da vida.* São Paulo, Loyola, 1991.

HACKMANN, G. (org) *Deus Pai.* Porto Alegre, Edipucrs, 1999.

JOSAPHAT, C. *Em nome do Pai, do Filho e do Espírito Santo.* São Paulo, Loyola, 2000.

KLOPPENBURG, B. *Abba: Pai. Deus Padre eterno.* Petrópolis, Vozes, 1999.

MARDONES, M. *Postmodernidad y cristianismo.* Santander, Sal Teresa, 1998.

MESLIN, M. *L'expérience humaine du divin.* Paris, Cerf, 1988.

MOLTMANN, J. *El Dios Crucificado.* Salamanca, Sígueme, 1983.

MUÑOZ, R. *O Deus dos cristãos.* Petrópolis, Vozes, 1986.

NOCELLI, G. M. «Matar o Pai?». In *Atualidade Teológica* 5 (1999), pp. 10-56.

PASTOR, F. *Semântica do mistério.* São Paulo, Loyola, 1982.

RAHNER, K. *Curso fundamental da fé.* São Paulo, Paulus, 1987.

RATZINGER, J. *Introdução ao Cristianismo.*
São Paulo, Herder, 1970.

SANTA BÁRBARA, L. G. C. *Notícias de Deus
Pai.* São Paulo, Loyola, 1999.

SEGUNDO, J. L. *A nossa idéia de Deus.*
São Paulo, Loyola, 1977.

SESBOUÉ, B. O. *O evangelho na Igreja.*
São Pauo, Paulinas, 1977.

SILANES, N. and PIKAZA, X. *Dicionário
teológico sobre o Deus cristão.* São Paulo,
Paulus, 1999.

SOBRINO, J. *Jesus, o libertador.* Petrópolis,
Vozes, 1996, pp. 366-390.

VON BALTHASAR, H. U. *Meditaciones
sobre el credo apostólico.* Salamanca,
Sígueme, 1995.

WAINWRIGHT, A. W. *La Trinidad en el
Nuevo Testamento.* Salamanca, Secreta-
riado Trinitario, 1976.

WAVISSERT, H. *La paternité de Dieu
dans un monde émancipé.* Geneva, Labor
et Fides, 1984.

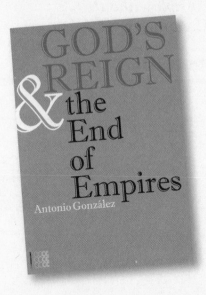

Reclaiming
the Spirit and Praxis
of the Reign
of God

God's Reign & the End of Empires

ANTONIO GONZÁLEZ
ISBN: 978-1-934996-29-4
384 Pages
Series Kyrios

González masters a vast variety of economic, political, sociological and theological issues with a high degree of scholarly command, clarity, and elegance. He offers a meaningful way forward and the courage not to lose hope —for those of us who have theoretically and academically struggled for quite some time with the structural, cultural, psychological, and overt violence of imperial capitalism… and for those of us who simply feel in our hearts that something is basically going wrong in our society, culture and world and are looking for meaningful alternatives. This is social theology at its best.

— Ulrich Duchrow, Professor of Systematic Theology at the University of Heidelberg

Antonio González, a leading Spanish theologian, was born in Oviedo (Asturias) in 1961. He has worked in El Salvador and in Guatemala at the Jesuit University, as well as in various centers of higher education in Europe. He shares with liberation theology the perspective of God's option for the poor and the centrality of praxis in the Christian message and life. He is a member of the Mennonite community and was the former General Secretary of the Fundación Xavier Zubiri in Madrid, Spain. González is a prolific author whose works include *Structures in Praxis* (1997), *Trinity and Liberation* (1993), and more recently, *Theology of the Evangelical Praxis.*

Post-resurrection communities continued to practice living in the reign of God. With the rise of Emperor Constantine, however, this vibrant counter-cultural movement of believers was institutionalized within the Roman Empire. Over time the institutional Church became the dominant power with all the trappings of empire. The author shows how regaining the practice of living in the reign of God can change the face of Christianity.

BUY IT AT: *www.conviviumpress.com*

Is Life in Society
Possible without
Morality?

Morality in Social Life

Sergio Bastianel
ISBN: 978-1-934996-14-0
360 Pages
Series Episteme

Morality in Social Life is a valuable work on the centrality of relationships, story, and virtue to morality in the social sphere. Those who are quick to advocate for public policies based on theological principles will be disappointed in this work, but they would do well to remember Bastianel's central thesis: ...God communicates himself in the man of Nazareth, in his gestures, words, his human way of living out relationships on this earth, in his living and dying, in his remaining present through the gift of the Spirit.

— National Catholic Reporter, Arlene Helderman Montevecchio,
    Director for Social Concerns, Gannon University

Sergio Bastianel SJ is currently professor of moral theology at the Pontifical Gregorian University in Rome and also serves as its academic vice-rector. He spent his early years teaching and lecturing at the Pontifical Theological Faculty of San Luigi in Naples, Italy, and in later years he served as dean of the theological faculty of the Pontifical Gregorian University.

Sergio Bastianel answers the question by addressing the responsibility of Christians to confront issues of justice within society in ways that promote the common good. The author, who views one's relationship with the «other» as foundational to the moral experience, places a priority on human relationships based on sharing and solidarity. He emphasizes the interconnections between personal morals and social justice and raises fundamental questions about such issues as political life and economics, about hunger and development, and about the true meaning of «charity», all of which are relevant issues in our contemporary societies.

BUY IT AT: *www.conviviumpress.com*

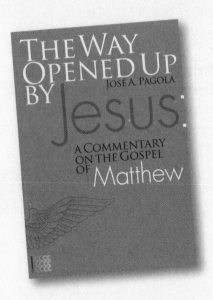

Rethinking
the Crisis in Ordained
Ministry

Builders of Community Rethinking Ecclesiastical Ministry

José I. González Faus
ISBN: 978-1-934996-25-6
176 Pages
Series Traditio

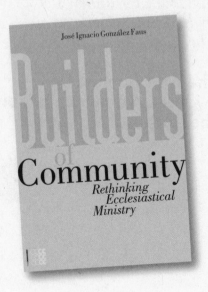

SCAN CODE
FOR MORE
INFORMATION
ABOUT THIS
BOOK

Gonzalez Faus's analysis and vision of the future provide hope for the ministry for the twenty-first century. He offers a formidable challenge to those who characteristically view the ministry as consisting of «power, dignity, superiority and remoteness» and offers hope to those who view the ministry as consisting of «service, surrender, sameness and nearness».

— Anglican Theological Review, Scott M. Myslinski

José Ignacio González Faus was born in Valencia, Spain, in 1935. He has a PhD in Theology from Innsbruck and is currently Professor of Theology and Director of the Centro de Estudios (Cristianismo y Justicia) in Barcelona. He is dedicated to the promotion and defense of freedom and justice within the framework of an integral vision of the human person. His numerous published works include *La humanidad nueva: Ensayo de cristología* (1974), *Acceso a Jesús* (1979), *El proyecto hermano: Visión creyente del hombre* (1989), *Ningún obispo impuesto* (1992) and *Where the Spirit Breathes: Prophetic Dissent in the Church* (1989).

It is exceedingly possible that the Church might be reaching what has been called «the time of the laity», and yet it is also possible that we might pass through this time in a sterile way, not because of not having known of its arrival, or what it was about, but because of not having understood the specificity of the ordained ministry and that of other ministries within Christian communities.

BUY IT AT: *www.conviviumpress.com*

*Rediscover the
Historical Praxis of Jesus
Through the Latest
Research*

Jesus. An Historical Approximation

José A. Pagola
ISBN: 978-1-934996-09-6
560 Pages
Series Kyrios

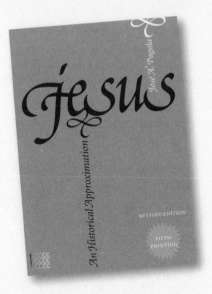

SCAN CODE
FOR MORE
INFORMATION
ABOUT THIS
BOOK

*This is an extraordinary work of scholarship. Beautifully written, it is also an expression of the author's
profound faith commitment… The author presents a compelling «approximation of that life»… A highly
readable book that deserves a wide readership in the Church and the academy.*

— Roberto Goizueta, Boston College, Former President of the Catholic Theological
 Society of America

José Antonio Pagola was born in Spain in 1937.
He completed his theological studies at the Pontifical
Gregorian University and his studies in Sacred
Scripture at the Pontifical Biblical Institute in Rome.
He also studied Biblical sciences at the École
Biblique in Jerusalem. He has dedicated his life to
Biblical studies and Christology and has done
research on the historical Jesus for more than 30 years,
selling more than 60,000 copies of his recent
theological bestseller *Jesús. Aproximación histórica*,
now available in English by Convivium Press.

This controversial book is now available in
English for the first time. In this bestseller, greeted
with both enthusiasm and controversy in
Europe, Pagola, criticized by some for depicting a
too-human Jesus, offers a scholarly and
thought-provoking biblical rereading of the life
of Jesus. Pagola reconstructs the complete
historical figure of Jesus with a scholarly exegetical
and theological approach, in an easy to read
language.

ERIC HOFFER AWARD
FINALIST

BUY IT AT: *www.conviviumpress.com*

A Face for God

This book was printed on *thin opaque smooth white Bible paper*, using the *Minion* and *Type Embellishments One* font families. This edition was printed in Panamericana Formas e Impresos, S.A., in Bogotá, Colombia, during the last weeks of the sixth month of year two thousand and fourteen.

Ad publicam lucem datus mense junii Sacri Cordis Iesus